THE UNBORN

**The Life and Teachings
of Zen Master Bankei
1622–1693**

Revised Edition

Translated and with
an Introduction by
Norman Waddell

North Point Press
A division of Farrar, Straus and Giroux
New York

North Point Press
A division of Farrar, Straus and Giroux
19 Union Square West, New York 10003

Printed in the United States of America
Designed by Thomas Frank
First edition published by North Point Press, 1984
First revised paperback edition, 2000

Library of Congress Cataloging-in-Publication Data
Bankei, 1622–1693.
   [Selections. English. 2000]
   The unborn : the life and teachings of Zen Master Bankei,
1622–1693 = [Fusho] / translated and with an introduction
by Norman Waddell. — Rev. ed.
     p. cm.
   Includes bibliographical references.
   ISBN 0-86547-595-4
   1. Rinzai (Sect)—Doctrines—Early works to 1800.   I. Title: Fusho.
II. Waddell, Norman.   III. Title.
BQB9399.E572   *99-089421*
294.3'927—dc21

Contents

Preface

Zen entered Japan at the time of the Southern Sung dynasty in China. Dōgen (1200–1251) began to promulgate his version of Zen, which, although it came to be called Sōtō (the Japanese pronunciation of the Chinese Ts'ao-tung), is in fact Dōgen's own Japanese Zen, which grew and developed around his main work, the *Shōbōgenzō*. The Rinzai sect, also introduced in the thirteenth century, brought to Japan the system and traditions of the Southern Sung Lin-chi school. Beyond that, it did not develop any characteristic Zen thought of its own worthy of mention. Later, when we come to the Tokugawa period (1603–1867), we see in the koan Zen of Hakuin (1685–1768) a new development in the methods or techniques of Zen practice and also, in a sense, a systematization of Zen thought. Slightly before Hakuin's time, however, Bankei appeared. His "Unborn Zen" espoused a fresh departure for the first time since the Zen patriarch Bodhidharma. Unborn Zen is truly one of the most original developments in the entire history of Zen thought. Bankei, indeed, must be considered one of the greatest masters that Japan has ever produced. (Daisetz Suzuki, *Studies in the History of Zen Thought: Bankei Zen*)

THE JAPANESE RINZAI PRIEST BANKEI YŌTAKU (1622–1693) did not leave behind any written exposition of his Zen teaching, and he gave strict orders that no one else was to reduce it to writing. But records were made nonetheless, his followers being unable to bear the thought that their master's words and deeds should go unrecorded and, as one of them put it, "just left for the sparrows to play around with." So although much more was lost than they were able to commit to paper, we must be grateful for the record they have preserved for us: it is our sole means of learning about his Unborn Zen.

This account of Bankei's life and teaching begins with an introduction tracing the course of his religious career. It is based on material compiled by his disciples and on references Bankei himself makes to his life in the course of his sermons. It has considerable interest as religious biography and should also provide readers with the background from which his unique Zen pedagogy emerged.

The remainder, and bulk, of the book is made up of translations from Bankei's records. Bankei is best known for the colloquial sermons ("talks" would perhaps be a better word to describe them) that he preached tirelessly to the eager students who came to him in great numbers from all over Japan. He delivered them in engagingly plain, everyday Japanese, the ordinary language of the common man. They are popular in the word's best sense. No one had brought Zen to the layman in such an informal and yet thoroughgoing manner. These vernacular sermons are given here virtually in their entirety. They are followed by an extensive selection from the records of the conversations Bankei had with the students and priests who came to him for Zen interviews, the teacher-pupil confrontations familiar to Western readers of Zen literature. Together, the translations of the sermons and dialogues demonstrate the basic religious standpoint of Bankei's teaching of the Unborn and provide a comprehensive picture of his style of Zen, which, in its genius, utter simplicity, and all-rounded wholeness, recalls nothing so much as the great Chinese masters of Zen's golden age in the T'ang dynasty.

Renewed interest in Bankei and his teaching has come about only in the last fifty years or so. It is due almost entirely to the efforts of the late Suzuki Daisetz. In a series of classic works published in the early 1940s, Suzuki clarified for the first time the true significance of Bankei's Zen and its high place in the history of Zen thought, rescuing Bankei from the obscurity of two and a half centuries of near-total neglect. Despite the literature that has grown up in the years since these studies appeared, Suzuki remains Bankei's best interpreter. His studies of Unborn Zen are, with few exceptions, the only ones that come to terms with its simple yet profound meaning. Anyone who studies Bankei must be deeply indebted to this great Zen scholar and teacher.

The work on these translations occupied me on and off for about fifteen years. Much of the material appeared in the pages of *Eastern Buddhist,* the journal of the Eastern Buddhist Society, Kyoto. I wish to take this opportunity to acknowledge a long-standing debt of gratitude to Dr. Nishitani Keiji, for answering patiently over the years the kind of question only he could answer. I am also grateful to Mr. Sugawara Yoshimune of the Kōrin-ji, for permission to use the self-portrait of Bankei reproduced on the jacket, and to the Futetsu-ji in Aboshi, for permission to reproduce the example of Bankei's calligraphy (the two Chinese characters *fu-shō,* or "Unborn") at the beginning of each chapter.

For this new edition, I have retranslated one or two paragraphs I felt stood in need of revision and corrected half a dozen or so misprints that had come to my notice over the years. I have also taken the opportunity to add a new section to the work. It is a translation of the greater part of *Unneces-*

sary Words (Zeigo), a collection of Bankei's talks and dialogues that had been represented in the original edition by
only a handful of entries. Now, twenty years after Bankei's
records first appeared, I can only wish that this new edition
will be received as warmly as the first one was. More than anything else, I hope it will convince a new generation of readers
that Bankei is, as that wise man Daisetz Suzuki pointed out,
one of the truly great figures in the history of the Zen school.

Norman Waddell
Boro-an, Kyoto, 1983, 1999

THE
UNBORN

Introduction

BANKEI YŌTAKU WAS BORN IN 1622, ON THE
eighth day of the third month at Hamada, a small village on
the shore of the Inland Sea, in the province of Harima, in
what is now eastern Hyōgo prefecture.[1] His father, Suga (or
Sugawara) Dōsetsu, was from the island of Shikoku; for generations the family ancestors had been physicians of samurai
rank in the service of the ruling Awa clan.[2] For reasons not
now known, Dōsetsu resigned this post and, as a masterless
samurai, or *rōnin*, crossed over the Inland Sea to the province
of Bitchū. There he married a Miss Noguchi and, after moving
twice more, settled finally in Hamada, where he presumably
gained a livelihood through the practice of medicine. Bankei
was one of nine children born to them, the fourth of five sons.
His boyhood name was Muchi, which translates roughly as
"Don't fall behind!" When Bankei was ten, his father died,
leaving the duty of raising him and the other children to his
mother and his eldest brother, Masayasu, who continued the
family tradition as a practitioner of Chinese medicine.

The records of Bankei's life reveal that he was an intelligent, highly sensitive child but at the same time rather unruly
and uncommonly strong willed.

His mother later told him that even at the young age of two
or three he showed a distinct aversion to death. The family
found that by talking about death or pretending to be dead,

3

they could stop his crying. Later, when he made a nuisance of himself by leading the neighborhood children in mischief, the same methods were used to bring him into line.

Every year on the fifth day of the fifth month, the occasion of the Boys' Festival, the village youths took part in stone-throwing contests, dividing into sides and hurling small stones at each other from opposite sides of a nearby river. This annual event had been held in the district for over five hundred years, since the Heian period, in order to inculcate manly virtues in young boys. We are told that whichever side Bankei was on invariably won, because he would never retreat, no matter how hard the stones rained down on him.

At the age of eleven, less than a year after his father's death, he was sent to the village school, where he took an immediate interest in his studies. But the calligraphy lessons, held after school at a temple in a neighboring village, were a different matter. For these he harbored an intense dislike. To avoid the monotony of copying and recopying Chinese characters from the teacher's copybook, he made a practice of returning home well before the class was over. Although Masayasu repeatedly took his young brother to task for this, his scolding had apparently little effect. In returning home, Bankei had to cross a river. His brother instructed the ferryman not to allow him to board if he should come along early. Bankei was not easily to be denied. "The ground must continue under the water," he declared, and he strode right into the stream, struggling along over the bottom until he emerged, breathless, at the far bank.

Wanting to avoid further conflict with his brother, Bankei thought of committing suicide. He had heard that eating poisonous spiders was fatal, so he swallowed a mouthful of them and shut himself up inside a small Buddhist shrine to await the end. Many hours later, seeing that he was still alive, he abandoned the attempt and went home.

At the village school, Bankei was subjected to the same curriculum as all Tokugawa schoolboys, the recitation of Confucian texts over and over until they came automatically to the lips. One day, the class was taking up the *Great Learning*, one of the "four books" of Confucianism. The teacher came to the central words, "The way of great learning lies in clarifying bright virtue."[3] Bankei interrupted the teacher. "What is bright virtue?" he asked. The teacher, repeating the glosses given in one of the traditional commentaries, answered, "The intrinsic nature of good in each person." Bankei asked what the intrinsic nature of man was and was told, "It's his fundamental nature." "Then what is that?" he persisted. "The ultimate truth of Heaven," replied the teacher. None of these answers satisfied Bankei. A deeper explanation was needed. He wanted to know what bright virtue meant in terms of his practical experience. This questioning marks the awakening of religious doubt in his consciousness, which was most likely already disposed in that direction because of the recent loss of his father. Bankei himself spoke of this critical juncture sixty years later as the beginning of his search "to discover the Buddha-mind." In any case, his questioning of bright virtue soon grew into an all-consuming passion. Fired by unquellable doubts, he embarked upon an urgent and relentless religious quest that would occupy the next fourteen years and determine the future course of his life.

At the beginning, he took every opportunity to ask others for help. A group of Confucian scholars, whom he pressed for an answer they were at a loss to give, suggested he try Zen priests, because "they know about such knotty problems." There were no Zen temples in the immediate vicinity, so he was unable to follow their advice. Bankei had to content himself with questioning more Confucianists and such Buddhist priests as he found in temples nearby. In addition, he attended every sermon, lecture, and other religious gathering that came to his attention. Afterward, he would run home and tell his mother what had been said.[4]

But such inquiries brought him no glimpse of understanding. He was unable to find a single person who could offer him any guidance. Thoroughly discouraged, he "wandered about like a stray mountain lamb, aimlessly and alone." Now even his schoolwork lost all interest for him, a development so displeasing to his long-suffering brother that Bankei was finally "banished from the family house for good."

Still only eleven years old, Bankei was on his own. If the records are to be believed, he does not seem to have been unduly troubled by this turn of events. On the contrary, he seems to have welcomed it as a chance to devote himself to his problem secure from all outside distraction. In any case, a close friend of the family, taking pity on him, stepped forward and offered him the use of a small hut in the hills behind his house.[5] Accepting the offer, Bankei wrote the words *Shugyō-an*, or "practice hermitage," on a plank of wood, propped it up outside the entrance, and settled down in earnest to devote himself to his own clarification of bright virtue.

The records are more or less silent regarding the next several years. He seems to have spent time at a temple of the Shin sect located close by. There he must have learned about that school's practice of the Nembutsu—the calling of the name of Amida Buddha. A reference in his sermons to long sessions devoted to the constant repetition of the Nembutsu—"days on end in a Nembutsu samadhi"—perhaps belongs in this period as well. When he was fifteen, Bankei lived for a while in a Shingon temple, where he presumably familiarized himself to some extent with the teaching and practices of esoteric Buddhism. The head priest of this temple, impressed by the young boy's resolution, tried to induce him to stay on as his disciple. Bankei refused the offer. "Neither the Shin nor the Shingon sect was to his liking."

The next year, having turned sixteen, he walked the twenty miles that separated Hamada from the city of Akō to visit the Zuiō-ji, a temple of the Zen sect that had been built twenty-two years before for the incumbent abbot, Umpo Zenjō.[6] Umpo belonged to the Rinzai tradition; his specific filiation placed him in the mainstream of that school, which traced its descent from the great Zen masters of the Kamakura period, Daiō and Daitō. Seventy years old when Bankei visited him in 1638, Umpo had earned a wide reputation as a stern taskmaster who demanded total dedication from his monks. A biographical notice of Umpo included in Bankei's records tells us that "few were bold-hearted enough to enter his chambers, and they usually fled before long."

Right off, Bankei told Umpo of the difficulty he was having in coming to terms with bright virtue. Umpo replied that if he wanted to discover what it meant, he would have to practice zazen, seated meditation. There must have been something about Umpo, and the Zen teachings and practice he embodied, that struck a responsive chord in Bankei, because then and there he asked Umpo to give him ordination as a Buddhist monk. Umpo, no doubt pleased to grant this request, coming as it did from such an obviously determined young man, immediately shaved Bankei's head. He gave him the religious name Yōtaku, "Long Polishing [of the Mind Gem]."[7] Bankei, the name by which he is best known, he acquired in his early thirties, when he served a term as a teacher in the training halls of the Myōshin-ji in Kyoto.

Although we have no specific information about the way in

which Umpo instructed Bankei, we can reasonably assume that Bankei was subjected to a demanding training program during the three years he was under Umpo's guidance. Zazen was, of course, the chief ingredient of training. Bankei probably did some work on koans as well, although no clear evidence reveals this and there is some indication that Umpo may not have laid the same stress on koans that his contemporaries did.[8]

At nineteen, after three years at the Zuiō-ji, Bankei set out, heading east, on an extended journey around the country that eventually took him throughout the Kyoto-Osaka area and as far west as the island of Kyushu. Once he took leave of Umpo, he had no fixed residence. He stayed in temples, but more often he lived a solitary life in rude, self-made huts, or, frequently, to judge from his records, he merely slept in the open. The privations of this life were great, but he faced them with a more than spartan disdain for hunger and extremes of season and temperature. He is reported to have lived among beggars for several years, first under the Gojō Bridge in Kyoto and later beside the Tenmangu Shrine in Osaka, where he slept with nothing but reeds for a covering. He sat for a week without eating at the Matsuno-o Shrine in the western part of the capital. From the following account by Bankei himself, we can form a picture of what his life was like at this time—although the disciple who cites it adds that it tells "but one ten-thousandth of the actual circumstances."

> I pressed myself without mercy, draining myself mentally and physically; at times, I practiced deep in the mountains, in places completely cut off from human contact. I fashioned primitive shelters out of paper, pulled that over me, and did zazen seated inside; sometimes, I would make a small lean-to by putting up two

walls of thick paper boards and sit in solitary darkness inside, do-ing zazen, never lying down to rest even for a moment. Whenever I heard of some teacher whom I thought might be able to give me advice, I went immediately to visit him. I lived that way for several years. There were few places in the country I did not set foot.[9]

When he went back to Umpo in 1645 after four years' ab-sence, Bankei was twenty-three years old and still no closer to resolving the doubt and incertitude pressing in upon him. He is said to have been weeping in discouragement as he told Umpo how he had been unable to find a single person in all his travels who could give him the kind of help he wanted. Umpo's reply was, "It's your desire to find someone that keeps you from your goal." He was telling Bankei that he would never be able to achieve enlightenment as long as he persisted in searching for an answer outside himself.

The words seem to have had their intended effect. Bankei promptly left again; this time he stayed nearby, building a her-mitage in the countryside to the north of Akō Castle. As if to underscore his determination to accomplish his end entirely on his own, he isolated himself completely from contact with the outside, walling himself up within his tiny dwelling. He sat constantly, day and night, dedicating himself with even greater urgency to zazen, resolved, just as the Buddha before him had been, not to get up until he had found the way through. Eventually, his buttocks and thighs became inflamed and swollen from constant contact with the bare rock floor. They began to fester. Still he kept sitting. He gave up eating for weeks at a time. He threw cold water over himself when-ever he felt even the slightest approach of the "demons of sleep." Here is one of several descriptions we have of his life in the hut:

The room, about ten feet square, resembled nothing so much as a prison cell. There was only one small opening, just large enough for an arm to pass through. The door he plastered shut with mud, so that no one could enter to bother him. Food was passed to him through the hole in the wall twice each day. After he had finished eating it, he placed the bowl outside the opening once again. A privy was arranged just below the wall, so that he could relieve himself from inside the room through a small aperture made for that purpose.[10]

But the long years of struggle had weakened him both physically and mentally. He contracted tuberculosis.[11] He tells of it himself in this famous passage from his sermons:

> The adverse effects of the long years of physical punishment built up and finally led to a serious illness. . . . My illness steadily worsened. I grew weaker and weaker. Whenever I spat, gouts of bloody sputum as big as thumb heads appeared. Once, I spat against a wall and the globules stuck and slid to the ground in bright-red beads.
>   . . . The illness now reached a critical stage. For a whole week, I couldn't swallow anything except some thin rice broth.[12]

The physician who examined him is reported to have "thrown aside his medicine spoon"—Bankei was past the point where such remedies could be of help. He was now resigned to dying. But with things at their blackest, his dramatic personal struggle to attain enlightenment came to an end:

> I felt a strange sensation in my throat. I spat against a wall. A mass of black phlegm large as a soapberry rolled down the side. . . . Suddenly, just at that moment, . . . I realized what it was that had

escaped me until now: *All things are perfectly resolved in the Unborn.*[13]

After fourteen years of incredible hardship, he had achieved a decisive enlightenment, his doubts and uncertainties disappearing like a dream. Immediately, he felt his strength begin to return. His appetite improved almost miraculously and with it his health.

Soon after this, according to the accounts given in two of the biographical records, another enlightenment occurred, occasioned when the fragrant smell of plum blossoms was borne to him on the morning breeze as he was washing his face in a nearby stream. One version of the story links this second experience to the first one in the following way:

The master, frustrated in all his attempts to resolve the feeling of doubt which weighed so heavily on his mind, became deeply disheartened. Signs of serious illness appeared. He began to cough up bloody bits of sputum. He grew steadily worse, until death seemed imminent. He said to himself, "Everyone has to die. I'm not concerned about that. My regret is dying with the great matter I've been struggling with all these years, since I was a small boy, still unresolved." His eyes flushed with hot tears. His breast heaved violently. It seemed his ribs would burst. Then, just at that moment, enlightenment came to him—like the bottom falling out of a bucket. Immediately, his health began to return, but still he seemed unable to express what he had realized. Then one day, in the early hours of the morning, the scent of plum blossoms carried to him in the morning air reached his nostrils. At that instant, all attachments and obstacles were swept from his mind once and for all. The doubts that had been plaguing him ceased to exist.[14]

When he was strong enough to travel, he made his way to the Zuiō-ji to tell Umpo what had happened. Umpo was overjoyed. "That is the 'marrow of Bodhidharma's bones.' From now on, no one anywhere will be able to touch you," he said, acknowledging Bankei's understanding. He told him, however, that he should obtain verification from other masters. Gudō Tōshoku, the most highly regarded Rinzai Zen teacher of the day, was the man Umpo recommended.

Bankei, who was now twenty-six, proceeded to the province of Mino (present Gifu prefecture), where Gudō's temple, the Daisen-ji, was located, midway between Hamada and Edo. Gudō, whose official duties obliged him to spend a good deal of time traveling around the country to the various temples under his supervision, was by a stroke of bad luck away in Edo, so Bankei could not avail himself of this eminent master's stock of experience. Having come that far, however, Bankei decided to try his luck with some of the other Zen teachers in the vicinity. What he discovered, to his disappointment, and a little to his disgust as well, was that none of the men he visited was in a position to give him the confirmation he was after. In fact, Bankei quotes in his sermons a confession one of these priests made to him, to the effect that what he taught people was not based on his own enlightenment (he really was not enlightened, he said); he merely repeated what he had learned from his teacher or what he had been able to grasp from his reading of Zen writings. He even praised Bankei for being able to see through his lack of true attainment.[15]

Bankei seems to have spent the next year or so in small hermitages built at different sites among the forested hills of Mino, as he applied himself to the important post-enlightenment phase of his training. He returned to Harima in 1650, where, into the following year, he apparently gave considerable thought to the course his future teaching activities should take. He contemplated, he says, "the natural capacity of my fellow men, and the means by which they could be instructed in the Way," trying to decide upon how best to transmit to others the understanding he had achieved.

In the autumn of 1651, while Bankei was still engaged in this period of reflection, news reached him of a Chinese priest by the name of Dōsha Chōgen, who had arrived from China and was residing at a temple in the trading port of Nagasaki in western Kyushu. Umpo proposed that he go to Nagasaki and see what the Chinese priest had to offer. Bankei, who was still eager to find someone to confirm his enlightenment, probably needed little urging. Leaving Akō almost immediately, he traveled westward by water, begging a ride on one of the small trading vessels that plied the Inland Sea, and arrived at Nagasaki a week later.[16]

Dōsha had landed in the sixth month of 1651. By autumn, the news of his arrival had reached Bankei's ears, and already, within another month or so, we find him in Nagasaki.[17] His initial interview with the Chinese master took place at the Sōfukuji, a large Chinese-style temple that had been built toward the beginning of the century on the slopes overlooking the harbor.[18]

During their first meeting, Dōsha confirmed Bankei's enlightenment, with the words "You have penetrated through to the matter of the self." After having said that, however, he added, "But you still have to clarify the matter beyond, which is the essence of our school."[19] To Bankei, who was brimming with self-confidence, this was inconceivable, so firm was his belief that he had attained great enlightenment itself, full and perfect. He thus refused, at first, to accept Dōsha's evaluation and told him as much. According to an account in Dōsha's recorded sayings, Bankei looked at Dōsha, laughed loudly, and then stalked brusquely out of the room without even making his bows. Still, he did not leave the temple. Instead, he stayed on for a few days, closely observing Dōsha and the manner in which he instructed the monks under him. Bankei soon realized Dōsha's true merit. He made up his mind to continue his practice at the Sōfuku-ji.

In the months that followed, he went often to Dōsha's quarters, where he no doubt had many spirited encounters with his new teacher. Since Dōsha did not know Japanese and Bankei could not speak Chinese, although he could read and write it, they had to communicate by means of *hitsudan*, the exchange of written notes in Chinese, "with brushes in place of mouths, and eyes in place of ears." Bankei took his place in the assembly and lived in the monks' hall with the rest of the students. But he was unwilling to follow some of the customs of the Sōfuku-ji, whose temple regulations were patterned on those in Ming Chinese monasteries. He was particularly averse to the practice of chanting sutras in Chinese. When Dōsha attempted to reprove him for not participating, Bankei replied that the Japanese had their own monastic traditions and customs, including those having to do with sutra recitation, and he could see no reason to adopt different ones now. "The only reason I've come here at all," he said, "is because I want to clarify the great matter. How can I afford to waste valuable time learning additional ways of chanting sutras?" Dōsha did not bring the subject up again. The toleration he displayed toward Bankei, here and throughout their brief association, is certainly to his credit and speaks well of his excellence as a teacher.

The following year, on the twenty-first day of the third

month, while sitting in the darkness of the meditation hall with the other monks, Bankei had another enlightenment experience.[20] He left the hall, rushed to Dōsha's chambers, took up a brush and wrote the question "What is the ultimate matter of Zen?" "Whose matter?" Dōsha wrote in reply. Bankei extended his arms out. Dōsha took up his brush, but before he could write anything, Bankei grabbed it out of his hand and threw it to the floor. He then "swung his sleeves and left."[21]

The next morning, Dōsha told the priest in charge of the monks' hall that "Bankei has completed the great matter." He directed him to move Bankei to the position of senior monk. But Bankei declined this distinction. He preferred his old place near the kitchen, and he continued doing his chores just as before, stoking the kitchen fires with fuel and serving the other monks their meals.

Some members of Dōsha's assembly seem to have resented Bankei's presence almost from the start. The biographies do not go into much detail here, but we may imagine that his independent attitude, which the others took as an expression of disrespect toward their teacher, had something to do with their displeasure. In any case, when they learned that the master had acknowledged Bankei's enlightenment, the undercurrent of resentment erupted into strong feelings of jealousy. As soon as Dōsha got wind of this, he called Bankei to him in secret and asked him to leave the temple for a while until matters quieted down, to avoid an incident with the others.

Thus Bankei, after a little over a year with Dōsha, put the Sōfuku-ji behind him and returned to his native province of Harima. From there, he proceeded to Yoshino, a sparsely populated area in the southern part of Yamato Province (present Nara prefecture); because of its inaccessibility, the area had long been a favorite haunt of the *shugenja*, the "mountain ascetics" of esoteric Buddhism. While practicing in a solitary hut amid Yoshino's high hills and narrow valleys, Bankei composed a group of simple Buddhist songs for the instruction of the peasants with whom he had contact. In them occurs the first recorded instance of his using the word "Unborn" in his teaching.[22]

From Yoshino, Bankei moved to adjacent Mino Province, where the following year, 1653, we find him back, after a five-year absence, at his small hermitage, the Gyokuryū-an, working hard further to deepen his enlightenment. The following incident is interesting for the picture it gives us of the confident young Bankei at the beginning of his teaching career.

Toward the end of the year, during the severest winter in memory, Bankei somehow knew, through a kind of second sight, that his master Umpo was gravely ill. He set out immediately for the Zuiō-ji to see him. At this time, a dozen other monks were living with him at the hermitage, among them a ranking disciple of the Zen master Daigu, by the name of Sen.[23] "How could you possibly know that your teacher is ill?" he said. "He's in Akō, many days from here."

"I know," said Bankei.

"*Hah!* You're a swindler, Bankei," scoffed Sen. "But if you're going, I'll go along with you. I've been wanting to pay Daigu a visit anyway." Midway in their journey, Bankei suddenly said, "The wife of an old friend of mine just died in Osaka."

"Fake!" said Sen. Since their path took them through Osaka anyway, the two men made straight for the house of Bankei's friend. The man hastened to the door to greet them. "Six days ago, I lost my wife," he exclaimed. "Strange you should come now. During her sickness your name was often on her lips. How extraordinary! Please come in, offer some incense for

her at the altar." Turning to Sen, Bankei said, "A swindler, am
I?" Sen stared in amazement. "After I've been to see Daigu," he
stammered, "I'm going to serve you as a disciple for the rest
of my life."[24]

Bankei did not reach Akō in time to see his old teacher. The
night before he arrived, on the eighth (or ninth) day of the
twelfth month, Umpo passed away at the age of eighty-five.
Just before he died, he gave his successor, Bokuō Sogyū, the
following instructions:

> I am certain that Bankei is the one person who is capable of rais-
> ing aloft the Dharma banner and sustaining the fortunes of Zen in
> the future. I want you, in my place, to push him out into the
> world. By no means should he be allowed to hide his talents.[25]

When Bankei returned to the Nagasaki area in the spring of
1654, with five recently acquired disciples in tow, he found
the situation there had drastically changed. The previous year,
the high-ranking Ming priest Yin-yuan Lung-ch'i (1592–1673)
had landed at Nagasaki from China with a group of twenty
monks. Unlike Dōsha, Ingen—to give Yin-yuan his Japanese
name—was there by official invitation and had been greeted
upon his arrival by a large delegation of important Japanese
officials led by the governor of Nagasaki. Relations between
the followers of the two men were strained from the start;
grievances arose, and it did not take long for strong feelings
of animosity to emerge. The Ingen faction, seeking to establish the primacy of their master's claim as the senior repre-
sentative of continental Zen, viewed Dōsha as a potential rival
and detrimental to their cause, especially when they noted
how successful he had been in establishing himself in Japan
and attracting a body of loyal students to his side. They seem

to have tried various methods of persuasion, and then pressure, to make Dōsha agree to become a senior disciple of Ingen's. When that failed, evidence suggests that Mu-yuan (Mokuan in Japanese pronunciation, 1611–1684), one of Ingen's chief aides, may not have scrupled to take stronger steps to discredit Dōsha's standing as a Zen master and make it difficult for him to teach in Japan.[26]

When Bankei learned of the troubles his former teacher had been having, he expended considerable effort on Dōsha's behalf to locate a temple where Dōsha could reside and continue instructing his Japanese students. He sailed to Hirado, to enlist the aid of the feudal lord Matsuura Shigenobu, who was himself a disciple of Dōsha's of two years' standing.[27] From there, he traveled to Kanazawa, a port in northwestern Honshu on the Japan Sea, a journey of from seven to ten days, in order to consult with Tesshin Dōin (1593–1680), a Sōtō priest who had been a fellow disciple of Bankei's at the Sōfuku-ji and was now master of a large temple, the Tentoku-in, near Kanazawa. But in the end, all of Bankei's efforts came to nothing. Although Dōsha remained in Japan for four more years serving as the incumbent of the Fumon-ji, the Matsuura's family temple in Hirado, he finally returned to China in the autumn of 1658. According to one account, he died on board ship on the trip back; another, probably more reliable source, has him dying in China in 1661 or 1662, at the reported age of sixty-one. Just before Dōsha set sail, Lord Matsuura asked him which of his students had really mastered the essentials of his Zen. Dōsha is reported to have replied, without hesitation, "Only Bankei."

The story of Bankei's life from this time on may be told rather simply. In 1657, four years after Umpo's death, Bokuō, in accordance with his master's dying wish, made Bankei his official heir. In addition to the Dharma Transmission he had already received from Dōsha, which linked him directly to that master's line of Chinese Zen, Bankei's formal filiation to the main Myōshin-ji branch of Japanese Rinzai Zen was now established.

The period of pilgrimage was over; while he kept to a rigorous mode of life, striving constantly to perfect his enlightenment, Bankei became concerned more and more with the spiritual needs of those people who were now coming to him for guidance in ever-increasing numbers. For the remaining thirty-six years of his life, he taught untiringly in temples and monasteries at a number of sites around the country; some temples were built for him by wealthy disciples, but he restored many of them on his own. Three among them served as centers for these efforts to propagate his Zen teachings: the Ryūmon-ji, in his native Hamada, the Nyohō-ji, in the city of Ōzu on the island of Shikoku, and the Kōrin-ji, which was built somewhat later in Edo.

The first of these, the Ryūmon-ji, the temple with which Bankei's name is most closely associated, was constructed for him in his thirty-sixth year, on a scale rarely seen in the provinces, from funds donated by a rich merchant of Hamada named Sasaki Michiya.[28] Sasaki was a boyhood friend of Bankei's; they had shared a desk at the calligraphy lessons young Bankei had so despised.

The Nyohō-ji was built in 1669 by Katō Yasuoki, the lord of Ōzu Castle.[29] Bankei selected a remote spot in the mountains behind the temple as the site for a small training hall, which he named Ōshi-ken, or "Heart-of-the-Matter hermitage." There, for two years in his early fifties, he isolated himself with a small number of handpicked disciples, totally cut off from contact with the outside world, in order to subject them to a continuous round of rigorous Zen training. He emerged from this sequestration only because of strong and repeated pleas from his many other followers around the country begging him to make himself available to their spiritual needs.

The last of the three, the Kōrin-ji, in the Azabu District of Edo, was completed in 1678 and given to Bankei by Kyōgoku Takatoyo, a daimyo of Sanuki Province, at the behest of his mother, the nun Yōshō-ni, an ardent convert to Bankei's Unborn Zen.[30] There, at the center of government, many important daimyo, their retainers, and high government officials came to take instruction from him and hear his lectures.

Journeying back and forth between these three temples, the Fumon-ji in Hirado, the Gyokuryū-ji in Mino, the Jizō-ji in Kyoto, and the forty or so other temples that he built or restored, Bankei devoted the remainder of his life to propagating his teaching of the Unborn and attempting to raise the fortunes of the Zen school, which for the previous century or so had been at a low spiritual ebb. In 1672, at the age of fifty, he was appointed the 218th head abbot of the Myōshin-ji in Kyoto.

From his late fifties onward, Bankei began to conduct extended practice meetings to make his Zen teaching more accessible to the great numbers of people coming to him for instruction.[31] During these retreats, he delivered his talks on the Unborn and held personal interviews with the participants, answering their questions and dealing with their doubts and problems. These meetings continued to be held until his death in 1693, usually twice yearly, summer and winter, for ninety days each. Some of them were limited to his immediate disciples, who numbered well in the hundreds, but many retreats were open to all and were attended by large crowds of priests and lay men and women of all ranks and denominations.

Among the countless men and women who flocked to Bankei during these final decades was Den Sutejo, a poet whose verses were held in great regard by her seventeenth-century contemporaries.[32] Den had become a Buddhist nun in later life, after the death of her husband. Bankei gave Den her religious name, Teikan.

Teikan's association with Bankei began in 1683, when she met him in Kyoto. Within a year, she had asked to become his disciple. The diaries she kept, covering roughly the last decade of the master's life, are filled with references to him and constitute a valuable source of information for these later years. Thanks to her, we know the dates of Bankei's travels, the places he visited, when retreats were held, and how many people attended them. Admittedly, much of that knowledge is obtainable from other sources as well, but nowhere else do we find descriptions such as the following, her report of the great Ryūmon-ji retreat of 1690. It is worth quoting in full, not only for the vivid picture it gives of this particular meeting but also for the prevailing mood she captures, which must have been much the same, though perhaps on a smaller scale, at the Nyohō-ji on Shikoku, the Kōrin-ji in Edo, or at any of the smaller temples at which Bankei held retreats during this period.

Since the retreat was planned at the beginning of the ninth month, only four weeks or so in advance, I hadn't expected many people to attend. But the word spread far and wide; they came from the far-off northern island of Ezo [Hokkaido], from Sendai and beautiful Matsushima, from the western reaches of Kyushu, and from all the home provinces; the news made its way even to the people in the distant islands of Ryukyu, for they were represented as well.

Many senior priests of the Rinzai and Sōtō Zen schools were

there, as were priests and nuns of all the other Buddhist sects, in numbers said to exceed several thousand. They were all gathered around Bankei's teaching seat, listening intently to the words he spoke, and devoting themselves in earnest to their practice. The names of the clerics registered on the attendance roster alone came to 1,680. In addition, great throngs of lay men and women had crowded into the western *Zendō* (Zen hall) and main *Zendō*, and new temporary halls were being put up daily to try to provide room for their ever-growing ranks. The streets of Aboshi were filled to overflowing with nuns and other religiously minded people from all walks of life and all parts of the country. Before we knew it, this little hamlet on the shores of the Inland Sea had been transformed into the capital of the realm, the very center of things. As all the houses in the village were soon full, storerooms, sheds, and every other available structure were pressed into service, even the barns, anywhere that would provide shelter for the floods of pilgrims. The villagers of Aboshi had never seen anything like it; down to the lowest servant boy and girl they were filled with the great excitement of the event.

Although the end of the year, the busiest of seasons, was approaching, no one took much notice of it, they were in such high spirits, overjoyed in the knowledge that they were able to be present at the Ryūmon-ji and hear Master Bankei preach.

The retreat finally drew to a close, but people were reluctant to leave. The old year departed, and when the new year arrived, there unfolded the truly memorable spectacle of thousands and thousands of men and women all crowding around to say their farewells to the master. No brush or tongue could possibly convey the sadness that was universally felt at having to take leave of him, and the great joy at having been a part of this totally unprecedented Buddhist assembly. Many faces glistened with tears of profound gratitude.

I can find no way myself to express the joy in my own heart, for being admitted into so fortunate a karmic relation as to have been born at a time when I could encounter Master Bankei, so like the Buddha Shakamuni as to be his very incarnation.[33]

The Ryūmon-ji retreat ended on the fifth day of the first month. After first making trips to Edo and Osaka, in late spring Bankei sailed with Lord Matsuura to the island of Hirado, one of the lord's fiefs off the western coast of Kyushu, and stayed there until the end of summer. The winter retreat at the Ryūmon-ji that year was limited to several hundred of Bankei's immediate disciples and as usual included both priests and laity. The following year, the winter meeting was held at the Gyokuryū-ji in Mino. According to one report, over six thousand people took part in the ninety-day retreat, which ended on the fifth day of the new year.

Bankei stayed at the Gyokuryū-ji for a few months after the meeting had ended and then proceeded to Edo, making several stops at temples along the way to fulfill requests for sermons. In the fifth month, he left Edo and headed back for the Ryūmon-ji, intending to make his usual teaching stops en route. It had been an especially hot summer, and the heat was severe. At the city of Hamamatsu, the master began to show signs of illness, and he decided to make straight for home. The litter carrying Bankei entered the gates of Ryūmon-ji on the tenth day of the sixth month. The following morning, he mentioned to one of his attendants that he would die within two months, but, to avoid causing alarm, he forbade him to tell anyone.

Among those who had been eagerly awaiting the master's return was Teikan. I will let her take up the story from here:

Tenth day, sixth month, Genroku 6 [1693]
Master Bankei returned from Edo. He became indisposed on the way and is very weak. Everyone is deeply concerned.

*Sermons on the fourteenth, twenty-seventh, twenty-eighth,
thirtieth, and first of the seventh month*

On the fourth day of the eighth month, he went to the western
part of the main hall to meet the nuns who had gathered there. As
I looked at his face, I felt my heart sink at the thought that this
farewell might be our last. He just came out, met us, and then returned to his chambers. Not a word was spoken.

*Sermons for three consecutive days,
the fifth, sixth, and seventh of the eighth month*

In spite of his extremely feeble condition, he spoke with great
patience and great attention to detail, as if he wanted to make certain everyone would understand the essence of Unborn Zen. I was
struck by the extraordinary sincerity contained in each of the
words he spoke.

Seventh day, eighth month

He went to his room after he had finished the sermon and remained there, resting quietly. He was not seeing anyone. Everyone
was asking about him in hushed and worried voices.

Summer this year had been particularly hot, even into the ninth
month, but it began to grow a little cooler, and I started to take
hope from the thought that this would be good for him. Then, at
about eight o'clock, on the third day of the ninth month, word
was sent to me that he had passed away. Deeply shaken, I immediately hastened to the Ryūmon-ji. I had prepared myself for the
worst, but now it was here. I could not help the tears that flowed.

At the temple, I asked the head priest, Sekimon, if I could see
the master and say my last earthly farewell to him.[34] "Certainly,"
he replied, and I was ushered into the room where the body lay. I
thought that the sight of his face would overcome me with grief,
but to my surprise, my mind was completely free of all such emo-
tion. My tears stopped completely. As I gazed intently at him, he

seemed just as he had been when he was alive: It was as if he were merely sleeping. How wonderful he looked, lying there with that kind and deeply compassionate countenance.[35]

Several months prior to his death, Bankei had stopped taking food. He had refused all medicines. He spent the time speaking pleasantly with his disciples. On the day of his death, he gave them some final instructions, and when he saw signs of sadness in some of them, he said, "How do you expect to see me, if you look at me in terms of birth and death?" Someone asked if he would compose a death verse, traditional in the Zen school. He replied, "I've lived for seventy-two years. I've been teaching people for forty-five. What I've been telling you and others every day during that time is all my death verse. I'm not going to make another one now, before I die, just because everyone else does it." After speaking those words, he passed away. He was in a seated position according to one account, lying on his right side, like the Buddha, according to another.

His body was cremated the next day, and, in accordance with his instructions, the ashes were divided; one half was placed in a funerary stupa at the Ryūmon-ji, and one half was taken to the Nyohō-ji and put in a funerary stupa that had been built there under Bankei's direction the previous year. At the time of his death, Bankei had as personal disciples over 400 priests and monks and 270 nuns, in addition to the more than 5,000 men and women of the laity who had received the precepts making them his students. They included people from all over the country, more than a few of whom were daimyo and other men of prominent position and family, as well as many students from the peasant classes. In 1740, forty-seven years after his death, the posthumous title of Daihō

Shōgen ("True Eye of the Great Dharma") Kokushi, or "National Teacher," was bestowed upon him by the emperor Sakuramachi.

NOTES TO THE INTRODUCTION

I have not given sources for all the quotations cited in the Introduction. They may easily be located in Fujimoto Tsuchishige's *Bankei kokushi no kenkyū* (A study of National Master Bankei), which is an exhaustive compilation of Bankei's biographical records, arranged chronologically in year-by-year sections.

1. Dates throughout are given as they appear in the Japanese texts, according to the lunar calendar. The lunar (Japanese) calendar is on average about five weeks ahead of the Western (Julian) calendar.

2. Until Dōsetsu moved to Hamada, his family name was Miyoshi; the name Sugawara was assumed after the move to Hamada, when he was adopted into a family of that name. Suga was probably used as a short form of Sugawara. Fujimoto, pp. 79–81.

3. Learning Confucian texts by rote was a method used in schools throughout the Tokugawa period (1603–1867). The *Great Learning* (*Ta-hsueh* in Chinese; *Daigaku* in Japanese), the *Doctrine of the Mean,* Confucian *Analects*, and *Mencius*, the "four books," were considered to contain the gist of the Confucian teaching. For its brevity and conciseness, the *Great Learning* was a particular favorite of Japanese neo-Confucians of the time, both those of the orthodox Chu-hsi school and those of the unorthodox Wang Yang-ming school.

4. Bankei's mother spent the latter half of her life as a Buddhist nun (her religious name was Myōsetsu), living in a small temple, Gitoku-an, in Aboshi, where Bankei always found time to visit her. She lived to the age of ninety, dying in her son's arms in 1680. The extent of Bankei's devotion to his mother and his deep commitment to the principles of filial

piety (albeit from his own Zen standpoint) can be felt throughout the sermons. In an entry in the *Gyōgō-ki* we read: "Bankei once spoke in a sermon of the sense of filial piety that he felt as a boy, which was responsible, he said, for his entry into religious life in the first place, and for his subsequent achievement of enlightenment. . . . Real filial devotion, he said, should not stop at merely caring for one's parents. A truly filial child should clarify the way of deliverance so as to be able to make his parents realize it too." Akao, p. 375.

5. This man is identified as Sukeshizu, the head of Shimomura village. He was instrumental in arranging for Bankei's father to be adopted by the Sugawara family (see note 2). Later, the great-grandson of this man, a Zen teacher in the fifth generation of Bankei's line named Daitei Zenkei, compiled a collection of anecdotes dealing with Bankei's life. This work, the *Shōgen kokushi itsujijō*, contains material Zenkei presumably obtained from his family's close association with the Sugawaras. Akao, pp. 415–16.

6. Information about the life and teaching of Umpo Zenjō (1568–1653) is meager, apart from what is found in Bankei's records. He began his religious career at the famous Erin-ji in Kai (present Yamanashi prefecture), under the master Kaisen Shōki. There, as a fourteen-year-old acolyte, he was close to a dramatic moment in Japanese history. When Kai was invaded by the armies of Oda Nobunaga in 1582, Nobunaga's men besieged the Erin-ji, and Kaisen and 150 of his monks were forced into the upper story of the monastery gate, which the soldiers then set ablaze. Before they entered the "fire samadhi" and burned to death, Kaisen is said to have written what became a celebrated comment in the annals of Japanese Buddhism: "When thought is annihilated from the mind, fire itself is cool and refreshing." Umpo escaped death because he happened to be away from the temple at the time.

After wandering for several years, Umpo ended up at the Sanyū-ji in Himeji with the Rinzai master Nankei Sōgaku, whose heir he eventually became. Later, he went to Akō, where, in 1616, he built the Zuiō-ji. According to a temple legend at the Zuiō-ji (Fujimoto, p. 97), when Umpo first moved to Akō, he worked as a common laborer. One hot summer day, a large funeral was held for a member of the wealthy Maekawa family. As the funeral procession filed to the cremation grounds, a sudden rainstorm came up; lightning darted all around, scattering the people and sending them scurrying back to the town for shelter. They returned after the squall had passed to find the "beggar-monk who had been hanging around the village" sitting atop the coffin doing zazen. "I couldn't let the Thunder God get hold of the body," Umpo explained, "so I stayed to guard it." This act earned him the gratitude and respect of the Maekawa family, through whose support he gained many followers, and led to the building of the Zuiō-ji.

Of his teaching style we know little, although Bankei wrote in an encomium commemorating the twenty-fifth anniversary of Umpo's death that Umpo "reviled the masters of 'word-Zen' infesting the land, crushed them into the dust, and promoted the silent, personal, and direct transmission of the First Patriarch, Bodhidharma."

Evidence suggests that Umpo may have served as the abbot of the Myōshin-ji (*Zen bunka*, vols. 10–11, Kōsai Kandō, "Umpo oshō no hito to nari ni tsuite" [The character of Priest Umpo], pp. 97–102). Despite evidence of Bankei's obvious respect for Umpo, there is only one passing reference to him in the sermons, and nothing to indicate that Bankei regarded him as his teacher. Rather he states repeatedly that, until Dōsha, none of the Zen masters he had encountered were capable of confirming his enlightenment.

7. *Kyokki*, Akao, p. 229.

8. A letter from Umpo to Bankei quoted in the *Kyokki* includes a report that he is teaching his students "by the direct method of the Buddhas and patriarchs, without the indiscriminate use of koans." Cited in Fujimoto, pp. 94–95.

9. Fujimoto, pp. 100–1.

10. From *Ganmoku*; quoted in Fujimoto, p. 104.

11. In *Dōgen, Bankei, Hakuin no ryōbyō tetsugaku* (The philosophy of treating illness of Dōgen, Bankei, and Hakuin), the author, Aoki Shigeru, investigates the lives and methods of practice of these three great Zen masters to determine what effect they had on the critical illnesses—diagnosed by him as tuberculosis—they all suffered from during their religious careers.

12. See translation, pp. 50–51.

13. See p. 51. While no doubt this expresses the essential import of Bankei's realization, it has been questioned whether at this point Bankei had arrived at this precise formulation—"all things are perfectly resolved in the Unborn"—which became a basic statement of his religious standpoint.

14. *Ryakuroku*, Akao, p. 349. A similar statement in the *Kyokki* (Akao, pp. 232–33) also attempts to link the two as separate satori (enlightenment) experiences. All the other records speak of only one satori experience at this time. Whether these references to two experiences are a later interpolation or not is unknown, but it is certainly possible that a second experience occurred, deepening the original breakthrough, similar in nature to those that came later in Nagasaki.

15. Gudō Tōshoku (1579–1661) is perhaps best known today as the spiritual great-grandfather of Hakuin Ekaku, the most important figure of Rinzai Zen in the past five hundred years. Called in his lifetime a "modern-day Bodhidharma," Gudō is credited by Hakuin with reviving and keeping alive the true spirit of the Myōshin-ji line at a time when it was in danger of dying out.

Gudō was enlightened under the master Nankei Sōgaku at the Sanyū-ji in Himeji—the same master from whom Umpo Zenjō later received his *inka*, or certification. He then went to Yōzan Keiyō at the Shōtaku-in (a subtemple of the Myōshin-ji) and became his heir; this places him, like Umpo and Bankei, in the Shōtaku branch of the Myōshin-ji line, which has been the most vigorous offshoot of the Japanese Rinzai school. In 1628, he was installed as the head abbot of the Myōshin-ji, the first of four terms in that office, and became a frequent lecturer at the imperial palace of Gomizuno-o (r. 1611–1629). Cf. Itō Kokan, *Gudō*.

The only record of a meeting between Bankei and this important master is a doubtful entry found in two of the biographical collections, which states that Bankei, after visiting several masters in Mino, proceeded to the Daisen-ji in Yaotsu to visit Gudō but found him "unsatisfactory." Bankei's own testimony, in the sermons, that Gudō was not at the Daisen-ji when he visited there should no doubt be accepted as the final word.

In the sermons, Bankei talks merely of visiting "several masters in the Mino area," without naming them; the biographical collections give them as Ryōdō Sōketsu (1587–1661), incumbent of the Daichi-ji, and Sekiō Genju (n.d.), founder of the Reishō-in (both temples are in the city of Gifu). The *Ganmoku* suggests a priest named Mitsuun Genmitsu (n.d.), identified as head priest of the Jikei-ji in Ōgaki, but this would be impossible in 1648, when Bankei visited Mino: According to Gudō's biographical records, Mitsuun Genmitsu's first interview with Gudō was not until 1653; he became his heir in 1657 and only after that moved into the Jikei-ji. *Gudō*, pp. 141–42. We may conclude, then, that Ryōdō or Sekiō, perhaps both, is probably the Rinzai priest in question—despite the fact that they were respected teachers and later head abbots of the Myōshin-ji.

The *Ganmoku* gives the following account of the conversation between Bankei and Ryōdō at this time (it may be compared with the one Bankei describes in the sermons; infra pp. 52–53): When Bankei found that Gudō was away, he visited his disciple Ryōdō. After listening to Ryōdō's recital of the Zen teaching, he asked him, "What about Gudō?" Ryōdō answered, "Gudō is just the same." Hearing this feeble answer, Bankei "gave up, and went away sighing, 'There's not a single true man anywhere in the groves of Zen!' " Fujimoto, p. 112.

16. Engelbert Kaempfer (1651–1716), a German physician in the employ of the Dutch East India Company, made the same journey from Na-

gasaki to Harima on his way to Edo in 1691, along the route we may assume Bankei followed. He took about a week to reach Aboshi and Akō, both of which he describes briefly. Kaempfer, vol. 2, book 4.

17. Dōsha Chōgen (Tao-che Ch'ao-yuan in Chinese; 1600?–1661?), born in Fukien Province, was an heir of the Chinese Lin-chi (Japanese Rinzai) master Hsueh-feng Ken-hsin (Seppō Kōshin in Japanese; 1603–1659). Ken-hsin was a brother disciple of Yin-yuan Lung-ch'i's (Japanese Ingen Ryūki; see note 26) when the two men studied under Fei-yin T'ung-jung (Hiin Tsūyō; 1593–1661) at the Wan-fu-su (Mampuku-ji) on Mount Huang-po in Fukien Province. Dōsha came to Nagasaki at an opportune moment; the priest whom Yin-yuan had sent from China to be the abbot of the Sōfuku-ji had perished in a shipwreck. The temple needed someone to fill the vacancy, and Dōsha was warmly welcomed to the post. During his tenure, he enjoyed considerable success in attracting talented Japanese students from all over the country. Besides Bankei, monks who went on to distinguish themselves were Tesshin Dōin, Chōon Dōkai, and Dokuan Genkō. Dokuan (1630–1698), who studied under Dōsha for eight years, supplies us with one of the few clues we have to Dōsha's Zen. It is found in his preface to the edition of Dōsha's recorded sayings (published in 1686) that he compiled: "He was not a great reader of books. The written word was not his forte. Yet when asked to, he could recite impromptu verses and Buddhist poems which were naturally tinged with the feeling of the ancient masters." Quoted from Nagai, p. 49.

18. In the seventeenth century, all of Japan's foreign trade—with the Portuguese, Dutch, English, and Chinese—was limited to the port of Nagasaki. Great numbers of Chinese, including merchants and traders, many of them refugees from the Manchus, lived in the city. To hold proper funeral rites for their dead, the services of Chinese priests were deemed essential. These immigrants constructed three temples, corresponding to the linguistic regions of China from which they came, and priests were invited from the mainland to serve in them: the Kōfuku-ji

(1620), called the Nankin-dera because it was supported by people from the Nanking region, was the first. Next was the Fukusai-ji (1628), or Chakuchū-dera; its parishioners were from the area of Chang-chou. The Sōfuku-ji (1629) was built by people from the Fukien, or Fu-chou, region—hence its popular name, the Fukuchū-dera. Kaempfer, writing in 1690, includes in his description of the life and institutions of Nagasaki a number of pages on the city's Chinese Buddhist temples, which are, he says, "remarkable for their handsom structure, and the number of monks maintain'd therein." Kaempfer, vol. 2, p. 147.

19. According to another account, the exact words Dōsha spoke at this time were, "You have penetrated through to the matter of the self, but you have not yet clarified discriminatory wisdom." Akao, p. 422. Buddhist wisdom may be described as having aspects of equality (or sameness) and difference (or distinction). The first of these refers to the realization of the absolute sameness of all things in the undifferentiated realm of emptiness; the perfection of wisdom, however, requires that such realization be deepened further, until one is able to return to the world of discrimination and form and use that realization in everyday life.

20. A disciple of Bankei's, Sandō Chijō, contends that Bankei merely had his original enlightenment confirmed in Nagasaki. Although Bankei himself does not mention this enlightenment at Nagasaki and seems clearly to have regarded the original experience in Harima as his decisive enlightenment, the evidence as a whole—from all the other biographical accounts, Dōsha's recorded sayings, and other sources as well—suggests that a further satori experience of some kind did occur while he was with Dōsha. Fujimoto, pp. 127–32.

21. Preserved in the Ryūmon-ji is a scroll on which are mounted two small slips of paper said to be those used by Dōsha and Bankei during this exchange. Although the wording of the question and answer that are inscribed on them is different from that given in any of the accounts recorded in the biographies, the general implication in the inscribed

version is essentially the same as that in the biographical records. Fuji-moto, pp. 125–26. That the paper fragments have been kept at the Ryūmon-ji, where presumably they were brought by Bankei, might indicate the importance he attached to this encounter with Dōsha.

22. Some of these songs found their way into print in 1769, under the title *Usuhiki uta,* or "Grain-Grinding Songs"; in some manuscript copies the title is *Honshin uta,* "Songs of the Primary Mind." In Yoshino, where they were sung to bring rain during the dry summer months, they were known as *Amagoi uta,* "Rain-Praying Songs." Fujimoto, pp. 139–46.

23. Daigu Sōchiku (1584–1669), a major figure in Rinzai Zen—it was commonly said he and Gudō Tōshoku "divided the Zen world between them"—belonged to the same branch of the Myōshin-ji school as Gudō and Bankei. Daigu's enlightenment came in a rather improbable way; he was doing zazen seated on a piece of wood that he had placed crosswise over the top of a well to gain some relief from the summer heat; the wood broke, and he fell, "head over heels," to the bottom of the well shaft. At that instant, his enlightenment "opened." *Daigu ihō,* p. 3. In his early forties, he served a term as head abbot of the Myōshin-ji, then resided for a time at the Nansen-ji in Edo; but his main teaching activity was in western Japan, in the provinces of Mino, Hyōgo, and Harima. In 1655, at the invitation of Matsudaira Mitsumichi, lord of Echizen (in present Fukui prefecture), he founded the Daian-ji in the city of Fukui, the temple with which his name is most closely associated. Bankei visited him there around 1655. His relationship with the old priest seems to have been marked by deep mutual respect. Accounts of several meetings and dialogues between the two men are given in Bankei's records. Akao, pp. 306, 424–25.

24. *Ryakki,* Akao, pp. 389–90. For a slightly different version of this story, see the *Unnecessary Words* section, pp. 181–82, below. Evidence of Bankei's supranormal powers of perception is seen in a number of entries in the records. After one of these entries, however, the editor adds that from his middle years on Bankei was never observed using

these powers because he feared his followers would misunderstand their significance.

25. Akao, p. 176.

26. Ingen, a onetime abbot of Mount Huang-po (Ōbaku-zan in Japanese) in Fukien Province, came to Japan as a refugee of the Manchus and founded a Chinese-style temple at Uji, near Kyoto, which he named the Mampuku-ji after the original temple at Mount Huang-po. The Ōbaku school of Japanese Zen that Ingen founded exerted great influence on many areas of Japanese cultural life. Mokuan succeeded him as the second abbot at the Mampuku-ji.

As Fujimoto has pieced it together, the story behind Dōsha's decision to leave Japan shows the Ingen group—at least some among them—in a rather unamiable light. Fujimoto presents all the available material, most of which admittedly has come from sources that would be expected to be partial to Dōsha. Yet he succeeds, I think, in showing that Dōsha was more or less forced out of the country by the maneuvers of the Ingen group. Fujimoto, pp. 157–66.

The following account of relations between Dōsha and Ingen is by a Myōshin-ji priest named Kōsai Soryō. It is found in a note he included in his unpublished edition of Bankei's sermons (compiled sometime in the eighteenth century). The scenario he describes can be corroborated in some but not all of its particulars from what is known through other sources. Even allowing for exaggeration, it seems at least likely that he does convey an accurate picture of the general situation that existed at Nagasaki.

Kōsai begins by quoting a dialogue between Ingen and Dōsha, which he says he heard one of Ingen's attendants report to his teacher Inkei:

Ingen said something to Dōsha, I don't remember what it was, but Dōsha replied, "I've been breaking in a good horse for twenty years. Today, I've been kicked by a little ass." Ingen got up and stalked out of the room. Later, still greatly angered by the incident, he said that he, a senior priest, had been insulted by a man who had only been wearing Buddhist robes for twenty years. . . .

Afterward, when Zen master Kōshin [Ken-hsin], Dōsha's master in China, sent him an official document that certified his transmission of the Dharma to Dōsha . . . Mokuan intercepted it and burned it to keep it from reaching Dōsha. He then accused Dōsha of teaching without proper certification. All this was to induce Dōsha to become a disciple of Ingen's. Dōsha would not submit. Other charges, equally unjust, were directed against him. They plotted to poison him but gave up the idea when their plans were discovered. From that time forth, however, Dōsha was confined to his place of residence—he was a man in a cage. So while he was physically present in Japan, it was as if he were not (since he was unable to pursue his teaching activities). Because of this, he returned finally to his homeland.

Kōsai concludes with this information:

Dōsha had a much larger following than Ingen did; there were at all times at least two hundred more people in his assembly. That, no doubt, is the reason behind the Ingen group's unseemly actions. Dōsha's assembly went about their practice simply and unpretentiously, while Ingen's tended to extravagance and ceremonious display. These ways have continued unabated, even until today. The Chinese priests [in Japan] have a tendency to be very self-assertive, always wanting to push themselves forward. It is little wonder they had trouble accepting someone like Dōsha. Fujimoto, pp. 165–66.

27. Lord Matsuura Shigenobu (1622–1703), whose ancestors had been trusted retainers of Toyotomi Hideyoshi and later sided with Tokugawa Ieyasu at the battle of Sekigahara, was himself a prominent

daimyo. He was noted both for his expertise in the martial arts, in which he was a student and close friend of Yamaga Sokō's (1622–1685), the greatest authority on military affairs of the period, and for his accomplishments in the tea ceremony, in which he was a pupil of Katagiri Sekishū's, and also the founder of his own school of tea, the Chinshin (the Chinese reading of Shigenobu). The island of Hirado, the Matsuura fief, flourished greatly as the center of Japanese foreign trade from the mid-sixteenth century, when the first Portuguese ships landed there, until the 1630s, when it was replaced by Nagasaki. The fortunes of the clan were thus sharply reduced during Shigenobu's administration, and he is credited with guiding it through the difficult times with sound economic and social programs.

Shigenobu became a follower of Bankei's shortly after the meeting described in the Introduction. The next year, when Bankei was living unnoticed among the beggars in the Asakusa District of Edo, he was discovered by one of Shigenobu's men who happened to be passing by and overheard a penetrating remark he made. The retainer reported it to Shigenobu, who invited Bankei to stay in a small hermitage within the precincts of his Edo residence. From that time forth, Shigenobu went frequently to Bankei to receive his instruction, both in Edo, where he was required by law to spend part of his time, and at the Ryūmon-ji, when he was passing through on his trips between Hirado and Edo. He also invited Bankei to teach and to lead retreats at the Fumon-ji, the family temple on Hirado.

28. The three Sasaki brothers are said to have been known throughout the country as shipowners. They were all active members of the Ryūmon-ji lay congregation. Akao, p. 914.

29. Katō Yasuoki (1618–1677), a direct descendant of one of Toyotomi Hideyoshi's most trusted retainers, was an eminent daimyo, noted as a master of the martial arts and author of several treatises on the subject. He also had a deep and long-standing commitment to Zen, having studied in his younger days with Gudō Tōshoku, from whom he

received his religious name, Gessō Koji, "Layman of the Moon Window." He was introduced to Bankei by Lord Matsuura at the latter's Edo residence; from then until his death, he was devoted to Bankei as a student and disciple and deeply attached to him as a friend. A number of their exchanges are recorded in Bankei's biographical records. Suzuki Daisetz has called their relationship "one of the most beautiful pages in the history of Japanese Buddhism." *Fushō Zen*, p. 15.

Yasuoki invited Bankei to his fief on the island of Kyushu in 1657, when Bankei was thirty-five years old (eleven years his junior), and presented him with his first temple, the Henshō-an. It was built in a forest of oak trees and could accommodate only ten or twenty monks. It was greatly enlarged twelve years later into a full-scale monastery and renamed the Nyohō-ji—a major undertaking, given the limited revenues of the Katō clan. Fujimoto, pp. 253–54.

30. Takatoyo (1655–1694) also built the Hōshin-ji for Bankei near the site of his castle in the city of Marugame and donated the land on which the Ryūmon-ji was built.

31. At first, these retreats were apparently conducted more or less in the traditional manner, with Bankei giving individual instruction to the participants; when the number of people reached the point where this was no longer feasible, the retreats turned into meetings for group practice, a prominent feature of Bankei's last decade of teaching. Altogether, there were fifteen such meetings, mostly during the winter months, from 1679 until 1693, the year of Bankei's death.

32. Den Sutejo, one of the most prominent women poets of her age, is known best today for a verse she is supposed to have written at the age of five: "Snowy morning/The character 'two' all over the ground—/ The tracks of the geta" (*Yuki no asa, ni no ji ni no ji no, geta no ato;* the Chinese character for "two" is two horizontal lines). The eldest daughter of a wealthy family in the Tamba area, she excelled in both the haiku and the waka form, studying haiku with Kitamura Kigin, the teacher of Bashō. She married at seventeen, bore six children, and was widowed at

forty, after which she became a nun of the Pure Land Jōdo sect. But after six years of study in Kyoto she found herself "still unsatisfied, with an emptiness of spirit." She visited Bankei at the nearby Jizō-ji, and when he returned to Harima, she followed him there, taking up residence close to the Ryūmon-ji in a small hermitage, which Bankei named the Futetsu-an. Her diary covers the period between 1681, two years before she met Bankei, and 1696, the year of her death. Fujimoto Tsuchishige's *Teikan zen-ni* (The Zen nun Teikan) brings together all the available material about Teikan and includes a photographic facsimile of her diary.

33. Akao, p. 568.

34. Sekimon Somin (1642–1696), the third abbot of the Ryūmon-ji, succeeded Dairyō Sokyō, Bankei's chief heir, who died in 1688.

35. Akao, pp. 572–73.

The Dharma Talks
of Zen Master Bankei

IN THE THIRD YEAR OF GENROKU (1690), AT the time of the great winter retreat at the Ryūmon-ji held under Zen master Butchi Kōsai Bankei, founder of the temple, the attendance roster listed 1,683 priests.[1] They came from all the different sects: from the two Zen schools, Sōtō and Rinzai, and also from the Shingon, Tendai, Jōdō, Jōdo-shin, and Nichiren sects.[2] Masters and novices alike and priests of every kind and rank gathered in a great assembly around the Dharma seat. The master might very well have been taken for the Buddha himself, as the teacher of his age and the master of all people and devas throughout the universe.

When the master came and ascended to the Dharma seat, he spoke the following words to the assembled audience of priests and laity.

I was still a young man when I came to discover the principle of the Unborn and its relation to thought. I began to tell others about it. What we call a "thought" is something that has already fallen one or more removes from the living reality of the Unborn. If you priests would just live in the Unborn, there wouldn't be anything for me to tell you about it, and you wouldn't be here listening to me. But because of the unbornness and marvelous illuminative power inherent in the Buddha-mind, it readily reflects all things that come along and

39

transforms itself into them, thus turning the Buddha-mind into thought. I'm going to tell those in the lay audience all about this now. As I do, I want the priests to listen along too.

Not a single one of you people at this meeting is unenlightened. Right now, you're all sitting before me as Buddhas. Each of you received the Buddha-mind from your mothers when you were born, and nothing else. This inherited Buddha-mind is beyond any doubt unborn, with a marvelously bright illuminative wisdom.[3] In the Unborn, all things are perfectly resolved. I can give you proof that they are. While you're facing me listening to me speak like this, if a crow cawed or a sparrow chirped, or some other sound occurred somewhere behind you, you would have no difficulty knowing it was a crow or a sparrow, or whatever, even without giving a thought to listening to it, because you were listening by means of the Unborn.

If anyone confirms that this unborn, illuminative wisdom is in fact the Buddha-mind and straightaway lives, as he is, in the Buddha-mind, he becomes at that moment a living Tathagata,[4] and he remains one for infinite kalpas in the future.[5] Once he has confirmed it, he lives from then on in the mind of all the Buddhas, which is the reason the sect I belong to has sometimes been called the "Buddha-mind" sect.[6]

While you face this way listening to me now, if a sparrow chirps behind you, you don't mistake it for a crow; you don't mistake the sound of a bell for that of a drum, or hear a man's voice and take it for a woman's, or take an adult's voice for a child's. You hear and distinguish those different sounds, without making a single mistake, by virtue of the marvelous working of illuminative wisdom. This is the proof that the Buddha-mind is unborn and wonderfully illuminating.

None of you could say that you heard the sounds because

you had made up your minds to hear them beforehand. If you did, you wouldn't be telling the truth. All of you are looking this way intent upon hearing me. You're concentrating single-mindedly on listening. There's no thought in any of your minds to hear the sounds or noises that might occur behind you. You are able to hear and distinguish sounds when they do occur without consciously intending to hear them because you're listening by means of the unborn Buddha-mind.

When people are firmly convinced that the Buddha-mind is unborn and wonderfully illuminating and live in it, they're living Buddhas and living Tathagatas from then on. "Buddha," too, is just a name, arising after the fact. It's only the skin and shell. When you say "Buddha," you're already two or more removes from the place of the Unborn. A man of the Unborn is one who dwells at the source of all the Buddhas. The Unborn is the origin of all and the beginning of all. There is no source apart from the Unborn and no beginning that is before the Unborn. So being unborn means dwelling at the very source of all Buddhas.

If you live in the Unborn, then, there's no longer any need to speak about "nonextinction," or "undying." It would be a waste of time. So I always talk about the "Unborn," never about the "Undying." There can be no death for what was never born, so if it is unborn, it is obviously undying. There's no need to say it, is there? You can find the expression "unborn, undying" here and there in the Buddha's sutras and in the recorded sayings of the Zen masters.[7] But there was never, until now, any *proof* or *confirmation* given of the Unborn. People have just known the words "unborn, undying." No one before has ever really understood this matter of the Unborn by confirming it to the marrow of his bones. I first realized how everything is perfectly resolved by means of the

Unborn when I was twenty-six years old, and since then, for the past forty years, I've been telling people about nothing else. I'm the first one to do this by giving the actual proof of the Unborn, by showing that the Unborn is the Buddha-mind and that it is always without any doubt whatever marvelously bright and illuminating. None of the priests or other people here at this meeting today can say that they have heard of anyone who has done this before me. I'm the first.

When you are unborn, you're at the source of all things. The unborn Buddha-mind is where the Buddhas of the past all attained their realization and where future Buddhas will all attain theirs. Although we're now in the Dharma's latter days, if a single person lives in the Unborn, the right Dharma flourishes in the world.[8] There's no doubt about it.

Upon confirming yourself in the Unborn, you acquire the ability to see from the place of that confirmation straight into the hearts of others. The name the Zen school is sometimes given, the "Clear-eyed" sect, stems from this. There, at that place of confirmation, the Buddha's Dharma is fully achieved. Once the eye that can see others as they are opens in you, you can regard yourself as having fully achieved the Dharma, because wherever you are becomes a place of total realization. When you reach that place, no matter who you are, you are the true successor to my Dharma.

A certain priest has said, "All you do is repeat the same things day after day. You ought to give your listeners a change. Their minds will be more receptive if you throw in some stories about the Zen masters of the past."

Dull-witted as I am, I think if I put my mind to it, I could probably remember a couple of anecdotes to tell people. But that would be like feeding them poison. I don't want to do that.

I never cite the Buddha's words or the words of Zen patriarchs when I teach. All I do is comment directly on people
themselves. That takes care of everything. I don't have to
quote other people. So you won't find me saying anything
about either the "Buddha Dharma" or the "Zen Dharma." I
don't have to, when I can clear everything up for you by commenting directly on you and your personal concerns right
here and now.[9] I've no reason to preach about "Buddhism" or
"Zen."

Despite the fact that you arrived in this world with nothing
but an unborn Buddha-mind, your partiality for yourselves
now makes you want to have things move in your own way.
You lose your temper, become contentious, and then you
think, "I haven't lost my temper. That fellow won't listen to
me. By being so unreasonable he has *made me* lose it." And
so you fix belligerently on his words and end up transforming
the valuable Buddha-mind into a fighting spirit. By stewing
over this unimportant matter, making the thoughts churn
over and over in your mind, you may finally get your way, but
then you fail in your ignorance to realize that it was meaningless for you to concern yourself over such a matter. As ignorance causes you to become an animal, what you've done is to
leave the vitally important Buddha-mind and make yourself
inwardly a first-class animal.

You're all intelligent people here. It's only your ignorance
of the Buddha-mind that makes you go on transforming it
into a hungry ghost, fighting spirit, or animal. You turn it into
this and into that, into all manner of things, and then you *become* those things.[10] Once you have, once you've become an
animal, for example, then even when the truth is spoken to
you, it doesn't get through to you. Or, supposing it does;
since you didn't retain it even when you were a human being,
you certainly won't have the intelligence as an animal to keep

it in your mind. So you go from one hell or animal existence to the next or spend countless lifetimes as a hungry ghost. You pass through lives and existences one after another in this way in constant darkness, transmigrating endlessly and suffering untold torment, for thousands of lives and through endless kalpas of time, and during it all, you have no opportunity whatever to rid yourself of the burden of your evil karma. This happens to everyone when, through a single thought, they let the Buddha-mind slip away from them. So you can see that it's a very serious matter indeed.

Therefore, you must thoroughly understand about *not* transforming the Buddha-mind into other things. As I told you before, not a single one of you in attendance here today is an unenlightened person. You're a gathering of unborn Buddha-minds. If anyone thinks, "No, I'm not. I'm not enlightened," I want him to step forward. Tell me: What is it that makes a person unenlightened?

In fact, there are no unenlightened people here. Nonetheless, when you get up and begin to file out of the hall, you might bump into someone in front of you as you cross over the threshold. Or someone behind you might run into you and knock you down. When you go home, your husband, son, daughter-in-law, servant, or someone else may say or do something that displeases you. If something like that happens, and you grasp on to it and begin to fret over it, sending the blood to your head, raising up your horns, and falling into illusion because of your self-partiality, the Buddha-mind turns willy-nilly into a fighting spirit. Until you transform it, you live just as you are in the unborn Buddha-mind; you aren't deluded or unenlightened. The moment you do turn it into something else, you become an ignorant, deluded person. All illusions work the same way. By getting upset and favoring yourself, you turn your Buddha-mind into a fighting spirit—and fall into a deluded existence of your own making.

So whatever anyone else may do or say, whatever happens, leave things as they are. Don't worry yourself over them and don't side with yourself. Just stay as you are, right in the Buddha-mind, and don't change it into anything else. If you do that, illusions don't occur and you live constantly in the unborn mind. You're a living, breathing, firmly established Buddha. Don't you see? You have an incalculable treasure right at hand.

You must understand about the marvelous illumination of the unborn mind. Once you have been to a certain place, you don't forget it, even after years have passed. It's easy for you to remember it. You don't always have to be keeping it consciously in mind. If someone else goes to that same place, the two of you will be able to talk about it, though you may be miles distant from it at the time. No matter where you are when you talk about it, it makes no difference; your accounts will still be in agreement.

While you're walking down a road, if you happen to encounter a crowd of people approaching from the opposite direction, none of you gives a thought to avoiding the others, yet you don't run into one another. You aren't pushed down or walked over. You thread your way through them by weaving this way and that, dodging and passing on, making no conscious decisions in this, yet you're able to continue along unhampered nevertheless. Now, in the same way, the marvelous illumination of the unborn Buddha-mind deals perfectly with every possible situation.

Suppose that the idea to step aside and make way for the others should arise spontaneously in your mind before you actually moved aside—that too would be due to the working of the Buddha-mind's illuminative wisdom. You may step aside to the right or to the left because you have made up your mind to do that, but still, the movement of your feet, one step after another, doesn't occur because you think to do it. When you're walking along naturally, you're walking in the harmony of the Unborn.

At these meetings, all I do is repeat the same things over and over again. But that shouldn't bother you, even if you've heard them before. It doesn't matter how many times you hear them. The more often you listen, the more certain you'll be of what I tell you. Every day new people come who haven't heard my talk before. Many will hear it today for the very first time. I'm obliged for their sakes to explain everything once again from the start. Otherwise, coming in somewhere in the middle of the talk, it would be hard for them to follow it and come to a real understanding of what is said. That's the reason why I say the same things day in and day out. Regular listeners will become surer of the teaching by hearing it repeated, and the new people coming all the time won't feel they are missing something. So each time I begin from the beginning, with the basics, explaining carefully and deliberately so that no one will have any trouble understanding.

People are here from every part of the country, members of all four classes of the Buddhist community: old and young, men and women, high and low, priests and laity. I see that priests seem to make up the largest group. Well, now that you're here, if any of you think you are enlightened, no matter who you are, I want you to come forward and let me confirm it for you.

I was twenty-six when it suddenly came to me that all

things are perfectly resolved in the Unborn. Since then, I've been trying to tell others about it. I've been all over. But from the time of that realization until now, I haven't found anyone anywhere who was a match for this tongue of mine. When I attained my realization, there wasn't any wise teacher around, or at least I didn't have occasion to meet up with him, so there was no way for me to get confirmation of my understanding. I had a very difficult time of it. I haven't forgotten the trouble I had, and so now, although I am not well, as you can see, I have made a great vow to do my best to give confirmation to anyone who is enlightened. That's why I come here every day and meet with you all. My own health ceases to be a concern. So if anyone thinks he or she has realized something, step out here and say so. I'll confirm it for you.

When I was thirty years old, my teacher told me that a Zen priest named Dōsha Chōgen had just come over from China and was now residing in Nagasaki.[11] He thought it would be a good idea for me to go and meet him. As I made my preparations for the trip, the master said to me: "You've managed to get by until now wearing layman's robes,[12] but if you're going to have an interview with a Chinese priest, you can't very well go dressed like that. Put on a proper priest's robe before you leave for your meeting with Dōsha."

So, wearing the Buddhist robes for the first time, I met with Zen master Dōsha. Right off, I told him about my understanding of the Unborn. He took one look at me and said, "This fellow is beyond birth and death." Dōsha was the only master at that time who could have given me even that much confirmation. Even at the time, I wasn't fully satisfied. I can see now, looking back to that meeting, that even Dōsha's realization was less than complete. If only he were alive today, I could make him into a fine teacher. It's a great shame. He died too soon.

All of you are extremely fortunate. When I was a young man, it was different. I couldn't find a good teacher, and being headstrong, I devoted myself from an early age to exceptionally difficult training, experiencing suffering others couldn't imagine. I expended an awful lot of useless effort. The experience of that needless ordeal is deeply engrained in me. It's something I can never forget.

That's why I come here like this day after day, urging you to profit from my own painful example, so you can attain the Dharma easily, while you're seated comfortably on the tatami mats, without all that unnecessary work. You should consider yourselves extremely fortunate, because you won't find a teaching like this anywhere else.

Just as I was foolish and bullheaded when I was young, sure enough, if I tell you about my experiences, some of the young fellows among you will take it into their heads that they can't achieve the Dharma unless they exert themselves as I did. And that would be my fault. But I do want to tell you about them, so let's make this point perfectly clear to the young men. You *can* attain the Dharma without putting yourself through the arduous struggle I did. I want you to remember that carefully as you listen to what I say.

My father was a masterless samurai, originally from the island of Shikoku, and a Confucian. He moved and took up residence in this area, and this is where I was born. He died when I was still quite young, and my mother raised me. She told me that I was a very unruly youngster and that I used to lead all the neighborhood children in making mischief. She said that from the age of two or three, I showed an aversion to death and dying. When I cried, my family could get me to stop by pretending they were dead or by talking about death. This method was also used to put an end to my mischief.

When I came of age, this being an area where Confucian learning was enjoying a great vogue, I was sent to a Confucian teacher. My mother had him teach me the *Great Learning* by the rote method.[13] When I came to the place where it says that the "way of great learning lies in clarifying bright virtue," I was brought to a stop by the words "bright virtue." I just couldn't understand what they meant. They raised doubts in my mind that remained for a long time.

I remember one day, I asked some Confucian scholars about bright virtue. What was it? What did it mean? But none of them could give me an answer. One of them said that knotty problems like mine were something that Zen priests knew about. He told me to ask one of them. He admitted that since he and his fellow Confucians devoted all their time to explaining the literal meaning of the Confucian writings, they didn't know what bright virtue really meant.

Since I was still no closer to understanding bright virtue, I decided to follow his advice. But in those days, there were no Zen temples in the area, so I was unable to find any Zen priest to question.

I then decided that, no matter what happened, I was going to get to the bottom of this bright virtue. I was also determined to tell my elderly mother about it before she departed this life. I groped about uncertainly, hoping to throw some light on the problem. I attended sermons and lectures. If I heard a sermon was being held somewhere, I'd run off immediately and listen to it. When I returned home, I'd tell my mother about what I'd heard. But bright virtue remained beyond my grasp.

Now more determined than ever, I finally succeeded in locating a Zen priest.[14] He told me that if I wanted to understand bright virtue, I should do zazen. Immediately, I took up the practice of zazen. I went into the mountains and sat without eating for seven days. Tucking my robes up, I sat directly on the sharp surface of the rocks. Once in position, without a thought at all for my health, I didn't stop until I could no longer sit up under my own power and toppled over. Because of where I was, no one brought food to me, so I often ended up not eating for days on end.

I returned home after that. I fashioned a small hut and shut myself up in it. I recited the Nembutsu and would enter a Nembutsu samadhi and go long periods without sleep.[15] I tried everything I could think of, but still I got nowhere. As I pushed myself past the bounds of physical endurance with this complete lack of regard for my health, the skin of my buttocks became lacerated, making it extremely painful for me to sit. But I must have had a constitution of iron in those days, because I was able to go right on without spending even a single day lying down to recuperate. To lessen the pain from my buttocks, I placed several layers of soft paper over the ground and sat on them, changing them frequently. Unless I did, there was considerable bleeding from the torn skin, and that, together with the pain, would have made sitting impossible. I also tried sitting on cotton wadding. Despite these difficulties, never once, day or night, did I lie down to rest.

The adverse effects of the long years of physical punishment built up and finally led to a serious illness. And I still hadn't clarified bright virtue, in spite of all the time and effort I had spent wrestling with it. My illness steadily worsened. I grew weaker and weaker. Whenever I spat, gouts of bloody sputum as big as thumb heads appeared. Once, I spat against a wall and the globules stuck and slid to the ground in bright-red beads.

The kindly people who lived nearby said that I should recuperate my health in the hut. They arranged for someone to look after me. But the illness now reached a critical stage. For a whole week, I couldn't swallow anything except some thin rice broth.[16] I became resigned to the fact that I was going to die. I viewed it as inevitable and felt no great regret. The only thing that really bothered me was having to die without discovering the meaning of bright virtue, which had had sole possession of my thoughts for so long. Then I felt a strange sensation in my throat. I spat against a wall. A mass of black phlegm large as a soapberry rolled down the side. It seemed to relieve the discomfort in my chest. Suddenly, just at that moment, it came to me. I realized what it was that had escaped me until now: *All things are perfectly resolved in the Unborn.* I realized too that what I had been doing all this time had been mistaken. I knew all my efforts had been in vain.

At the same time, my illness showed definite signs of improvement. Overjoyed, I found that my appetite had returned. I called to the nurse, told him I thought I could eat something, and asked him to prepare some rice gruel. While he seemed to think it a strange request coming from someone at death's door, he was delighted and hurriedly began to prepare the food. In his eagerness to feed me as quickly as possible, he gave me the gruel before the rice had been cooked through. But I didn't even notice. I wolfed down two or three bowls of it without suffering any adverse effects. From that point on, I improved steadily, and here I am, still alive today. I was able to fulfill my vow after all and also to bring my mother to an understanding of the Unborn.

From that time until today, I have encountered no one anywhere who could disprove my teaching. If only I had encountered someone with a real understanding of the Dharma to speak with while I was traveling around from place to place struggling with my problem, I wouldn't have had to expend all that useless effort. But there was no such person, and I practiced prolonged and painful austerities, subjecting my body to hardships so severely punishing that I suffer from the effects even today. That's the reason I'm not able to come here and meet with you as often as I would like.

Well, after I realized that all things are resolved by means of the Unborn, I wanted to talk to someone about it. As I was considering whom I should visit, my master told me of a priest named Gudō, in Mino Province.[17] He described him as an excellent teacher and advised me to go and have an interview with him. I followed his advice and traveled to Mino, but Gudō was away in Edo at the time, and I was unable to meet and talk with him. Having already come that far, however, I thought that, rather than return with nothing to show for my trip, I would visit some of the other Zen priests in the area.[18]

I introduced myself to one of them as a Zen monk from Harima Province and told him that I had come all that distance to receive his instruction. He explained the Zen teaching to me. After he had finished, I said: "I realize that it's very disrespectful for me to speak at all, but I would like to say something. Please forgive the lack of propriety.

"All that you and everyone else here has said to me is very true. It's not that I don't agree with it. Only, somehow or other, the feeling I get is that of scratching an itchy foot with my shoe on. It's not getting to the itch. Your teachings don't strike home to the center, to the real marrow."

Surprisingly enough, my words didn't disconcert him in the least. He answered: "Of course. It's just as you say. We teach others in the same manner we ourselves have been taught. We just follow the teachings of previous masters, which are found written down in sutras and Zen records. I'm ashamed to say it, but the fact is that what we teach isn't really based on enlightenment. Since we're not really enlightened, it's understandable that you should say what you do about our teaching not being able to reach the place that itches. You were able to see through all that and recognize me for what I am. Surely, you're no ordinary man."

Naturally, under those circumstances, it was impossible to get verification from any of them. I returned home and shut myself up in retreat again. It was then, as I was engaged in contemplating the natural capacity of my fellow men and the means by which they could be instructed in the Way, that I heard about Dōsha having come to Nagasaki. I went at the suggestion of my teacher Umpo and visited him, and, as I've told you all before, he confirmed my understanding. I really had a hard time finding someone able to give positive verification of my enlightenment. There just wasn't anybody.

I appear here every day to talk with you for that very reason. If any of you come to enlightenment, you're fortunate to have someone around to give you verification of it. If you believe you've reached enlightenment, then you should say so. Otherwise, you should listen carefully and confirm what I say for yourselves. Then you will be enlightened. When you speak of a "Buddha," or a "patriarch," that is merely a name. It is a word that is left behind after they appear or are "born" and is several removes from the site of the Unborn itself—and thus totally unimportant. When you dwell in the Unborn itself, you're dwelling at the very wellhead of the Buddhas and patriarchs. No one can know the dwelling place of a person who is firmly convinced that the Buddha-mind is Unborn. It isn't known even to Buddhas and patriarchs.

If you establish yourself firmly in the Unborn, then simply

and without any trouble or effort, while sitting comfortably on the tatami mats, you're an authentic Tathagata, a *living* Buddha. The eye to see others will open in you, and you'll be able to see everything from the vantage point of realization. I never err in my judgment of people, nor does anyone else who has the eye of the Unborn. Our school has been called the "Cleareyed" sect for that reason. And, since this ability is possible because you're dwelling in the unborn Buddha-mind, it is sometimes called the "Buddha-mind" sect as well. When the eye to see others opens in you, and you can see straight into their hearts, you may consider that you've fully realized the Buddha's Dharma, because then, at that very place, that's just what you've done.

Until you realize for yourselves what I've just said, you may find it hard to believe. You may even think I'm trying to deceive you. But after you leave here, when the day comes that you do realize it, that very day and at that very spot, whoever you are, you too will be able to see into others' hearts. You'll know then that everything I've said is true. Be diligent now, in the interests of that future day. If I were lying to you, my tongue would be pulled out after I die for the sin of speaking falsehood. Do you think I'd be standing here telling you lies, knowing that I'd fall into the tongue-pulling hell for doing it?[19]

The unborn Dharma disappeared in both Japan and China, and it has long since been forgotten. But now it has appeared in the world again. Once you come to be convinced that unborn, illuminating wisdom is unmistakably the Buddha-mind, your belief in it becomes unshakable. Then it's as if all the people in the world were to get together and try to make you believe that a crow was a heron. Since you know very well by your common experience that a crow is by nature black and a heron white, they couldn't convince you no matter how hard or how long they tried.

Once you come to know without any doubt that the marvelous illuminative wisdom of the Unborn is the Buddhamind and that the Buddha-mind puts all things in perfect order by means of the Unborn, then you can no longer be deluded or led astray by others. People with this unshakable conviction are called "the firm and incontrovertible." For today and for endless future ages, they are unborn, living Buddhas.

When I was young and first began to declare the unborn Dharma, people had trouble understanding it. They thought I was preaching heresy, or they took me for a Christian.[20] They were afraid of me. No one would come near. But it wasn't long before they realized their mistake and came to know perfectly well that I was teaching them the true Dharma. Now, instead of their staying away as before, I'm besieged by too many callers, imploring and pressing me to meet with them. I don't have a moment to myself.

All things have their season. Since I first came to live in this temple, more than forty years have passed, and because I've been repeating my teaching over and over during that time, many people can be found in these parts who excel the masters of religion.

Your self-partiality is at the root of all your illusions. There aren't any illusions when you don't have this preference for yourself. If the men sitting next to you start quarreling, it may be easy for you to tell which of the disputants is in the right and which in the wrong, because you're not involved yourself. You are a bystander, so you can keep a cool head. But what if

you do have a part in it? Then you take your own side and oppose the other fellow. As you fight with each other, you transform your Buddha-minds into fighting spirits.

Or again, because of the Buddha-mind's wonderful illuminative wisdom, such things as you have done and experienced
in the past cannot fail to be reflected in it. If you fix onto
those images as they reflect, you are unwittingly creating illusion. The thoughts do not already exist at the place where
those images are reflecting; they are caused by your past experiences and occur when things you have seen and heard in
the past are reflected on the Buddha-mind. But thoughts originally have no real substance. So if they are reflected, you
should just let them be reflected, and let them arise when
they arise. Don't have any thought to stop them. If they stop,
let them stop. Don't pay any attention to them. Leave them
alone. Then illusions won't appear. And since there are no illusions when you don't take note of the reflecting images,
while the images may be reflected in the mind, it's just the
same as if they weren't. A thousand thoughts may arise, yet it's
just as though they hadn't. They won't give you a bit of trouble. You won't have any thoughts to clear from your mind—
not a single thought to cut off.

Bankei spoke to the assembly on the first day of the twelfth
month:[21] At my temples, every moment, day and night, is the
fixed and appointed time for practice. I don't do as they do
elsewhere and tell you that the period of practice begins at
such and such a time. Everyone doesn't start dashing around
making a great fuss.

There was once a monk in my temple who had been doz-
ing off. Another monk saw him and really laid into him with a
stick. I reprimanded him: "Why hit him when he's enjoying a

pleasant nap? Do you think he leaves the Buddha-mind and goes somewhere else when he sleeps?" Now, I don't urge people to sleep around here. But once they are asleep, you're making a serious mistake if you hit them. Nothing like that is allowed to happen here anymore. We don't go out of our way to urge people to take naps. Yet neither do we hit them or scold them for it if they do. We don't scold them or praise them for sleeping, any more than we scold them or praise them for not sleeping.

If you stay awake, you stay awake. If you sleep, you sleep. When you sleep, you sleep in the same Buddha-mind you were awake in. When you're awake, you're awake in the same Buddha-mind you were sleeping in. You sleep in the Buddha-mind while you sleep and are up and about in the Buddha-mind while you're up and about. That way, you always stay in the Buddha-mind. You're never apart from it for an instant.

You're wrong if you think that people become something different when they fall asleep. If they were in the Buddha-mind only during their waking hours and changed into something else when they went to sleep, that wouldn't be the true Buddhist Dharma. It would mean that they were always in a state of transmigration.

All of you people here are working hard to become Buddhas. That's the reason you want to scold and beat the ones who fall asleep. But it isn't right. You each received one thing from your mother when you were born—the unborn Buddha-mind. Nothing else. Rather than try to become a Buddha, when you just stay constantly in the unborn mind, sleeping in it when you sleep, up and about in it when you're awake, you're a living Buddha in your everyday life—at all times. There's not a moment when you're not a Buddha. Since you're always a Buddha, there's no other Buddha in addition to that for you to become. Instead of trying to *become* a Buddha, then, a much easier and shorter way is just to *be* a Buddha.

The unborn Buddha-mind deals freely and spontaneously with anything that presents itself to it. But if something should happen to make you change the Buddha-mind into thought, then you run into trouble and lose that freedom. Let me give you an example. Suppose a woman is engaged in sewing something. A friend enters the room and begins speaking to her. As long as she listens to her friend and sews in the Unborn, she has no trouble doing both. But if she gives her attention to her friend's words and a thought arises in her mind as she thinks about what to reply, her hands stop sewing; if she turns her attention to her sewing and thinks about that, she fails to catch everything her friend is saying, and the conversation does not proceed smoothly. In either case, her Buddha-mind has slipped from the place of the Unborn. She has transformed it into thought. As her thoughts fix upon one thing, they're blank to all others, depriving her mind of its freedom.

Let me tell you about what happened when I was in Marugame in Sanuki Province. As you know, Marugame is a castle town, and when I was there, many people came to listen to the talks. On one occasion, a lady showed up, accompanied by her maidservant and an elderly woman. The three of them listened and then left. Sometime afterward, the lady and the old woman came again. The lady said: "Before she met you, my elderly attendant here was always a willful and disagreeable creature. She would lose her temper at the slightest pretext. But you know, it's been quite a while now since we heard your teaching, and from that time till the present day, she hasn't once been ill-tempered. In fact, she's grown most wise. Everything she says is sensible and sound. She doesn't seem to have a foolish notion in her head. She's put me to shame with the example she's set. I'm certain that the reason for the change in her is simply that she's taken your teaching straight to heart. We owe it all to your influence."

Such were her words, and from what I learned later, the old woman never strayed from the Buddha-mind again.

What I call the "Unborn" is the Buddha-mind. This Buddha-mind is unborn, with a marvelous virtue of illuminative wisdom. In the Unborn, all things fall right into place and remain in perfect harmony. When everything you do is done according to the Unborn, the eye that sees others as they are opens in you, and you know in your own mind that everyone you see is a living Buddha. That's the reason why once you live in the Unborn you never fall back into your old ways, just like that old woman of Sanuki. Once you know the great worth of the Buddha-mind, you can't leave it for illusion again. But as long as you're ignorant of its great value, you will continue to create illusions for yourself in whatever you do, insignificant things included, and you will live as an unenlightened person.

I notice that there are many ladies here today. Compared with men, you women tend to get excited easily. Even unimportant things are enough to upset you and turn your unborn Buddha-mind into a fighting spirit, ignorant animal, or craving hungry ghost, submerging you in illusion and causing you to transmigrate into many different forms. You should pay particular attention to everything I say.

In the houses with domestic help, servant boys and girls

are employed in large numbers. Some among them are bound to be careless with things. Occasionally, treasured dishes or other articles are broken. Perhaps it is something not even worth mentioning, but in any case, you let the blood rush to your head. You lash out and scold the offender angrily. But no matter how prized the dish or tea bowl may have been, it wasn't broken deliberately. It was an accident, and now there's nothing that can be done about it. Just the same, you fly into a rage and let the defilements from your self-centered passions transform the precious Buddha-mind given when you were born into a fighting spirit. You can always buy another teacup. Tea tastes the same anyway, whether from an ordinary Imari teacup or from a priceless Korean tea bowl. You can drink it just as well from either one. But a temper, once lost, can't easily be undone.

Now, if you really understand what I've been saying about the tea bowl, you should know, without my having to tell you about them one by one, that it's the same for everything else. Whatever happens, just don't turn your Buddha-minds into fighting spirits by worrying over it. Don't change them into ignorance or let your self-centered thoughts turn them into hungry ghosts. Then you'll automatically be living in the unborn Buddha-mind. You won't have any choice in the matter. Once you know the Buddha-mind's great value, there's no way you can avoid dwelling in the Unborn even if you don't want to. I want to make you know how vitally important it is for you not to change your Buddha-minds into the three poisons,[22] so you will have to listen to me attentively and then be very careful that you don't transform your Buddha-minds into something else.

When I tell people about the Unborn like this, they sometimes assume it's a teaching I came up with all by myself. But that's mistaken. If you look through the sutras and other Buddhist records, you'll find that the Unborn was preached in the past in various ways.[23] The patriarchs of the Zen school mentioned it. It was heard from the golden mouth of Shakamuni himself. Even children have known of it. But it's always the *words* "unborn, undying" that you find. There's never any verification given to show just what this "unborn, undying" really is. I am the first to teach people by giving them proof of the Unborn. It's understandable, then, that those who don't know this should make the mistake of thinking that I thought the words up myself.

As a young man striving to realize the Buddha-mind, I tried my hand at koan study. I had interviews with Zen teachers and engaged in Zen dialogues with them in Chinese. I worked very diligently at it. But it is better for us Japanese to use the common language we speak every day when we ask questions having to do with the Way. Since we aren't very good at Chinese, when we have to use it for such questions and answers, we have trouble expressing ourselves fully and saying just what we want to. But if we use our own everyday language and speak just the way we normally do, there's nothing at all we can't ask about. Instead of straining around worrying about how to ask something in Chinese, we should ask our questions in a language we can use easily, free of the burdens and constraints of a foreign language. Of course, if we couldn't attain realization unless we used Chinese, I would be the first to say use it. But the fact is that we can ask about the Way, and attain it, without any trouble at all by using our own language. It's wrong for us to have to ask questions in a language we have difficulty using. You must remember this, and whenever you have something to ask me, feel no hesitation. I don't care what it is, ask it just the way you want to, in your own words, and I'll help you clear it up. Since you're able to resolve things in that way, what could be as useful to you and convenient to use as the ordinary Japanese you speak every day?

While I was studying with Dōsha in Nagasaki, a letter was sent to China to the priest Ingen, inviting him to come to Nagasaki.[24] I was one of those who took part in the discussions leading up to the issuance of that invitation, and, fortunately, I happened to be visiting Dōsha when Ingen finally arrived. As his boat sailed to the port entrance, all the monks in Dōsha's assembly went down to the quay to welcome him. But when Ingen disembarked the ship, I knew the moment I set eyes on him that he wasn't a man of the Unborn. So I never bothered to go to him for instruction.

People generally have the wrong idea about living and dying at will. They think it means that someone decides on one day that he will die on the next, or that he predicts the day and month in the following year when he is to die and then does indeed die a natural death on that date, or they think it means the ability to extend one's lifetime so many days or months. Such are the notions many people have. I myself won't say that they aren't examples of living and dying at will; obviously, in a sense, such people do live and die very much at will. But since their ability is the result of training and practice, it's sometimes seen even in those whose religious eye has not yet been opened. Even some nonreligious people may know when they're going to die. But in such cases, since their religious eye is not opened, they don't have the slightest idea of its real meaning.

A man of the Unborn is beyond living and dying (samsara).

What I mean by that is: Someone who is unborn is also undying, so he is beyond both birth and death. What *I* call living and dying at will is when someone dies without being troubled by life and death, the continuous succession of birth-death, birth-death that is samsaric existence. Moreover, living and dying is taking place at every instant throughout the twenty-four hours of the day; dying does not occur only once in your life when you cease breathing. When you're living without being concerned about life or death, you're always living in such a way that whenever death does come, even right now, at this moment, it's no great matter. Now, that's what I call "living and dying at will." It means living confirmed in your unborn Buddha-mind. To make a declaration that you'll die at a certain time on a certain fixed day and to have that on your mind—can you imagine how confining and unfree that would be?

You often hear religious people talking about samsara, or living and dying, being the same as nirvana.[25] But when they speak about it, they do so from the standpoint of samsara, so in fact it has nothing to do with nirvana. They make this mistake because they haven't grasped yet that the unborn Buddha-mind they always have with them sets everything right this very day by means of the Unborn. To look for "samsara is nirvana" anywhere else and involve yourself in words and letters is pointless. What they're doing is changing the unborn Buddha-mind into the thought "samsara is nirvana" and senselessly spending every second of the day and night, without a moment's rest, confined within samsara. Since the Buddha-mind takes care of everything by means of the Unborn, it has nothing to do with samsara or nirvana. Seen from the place of the Unborn, both of them are like the shadows in a dream. But because the Buddha-mind has the marvelous dexterity it does, if a person who until just yesterday was busily engaged in samsara should today realize his mistake and henceforth stop changing his Buddha-mind into the three poisons, he will henceforth dwell in the Buddha-mind free of all concern with such things as samsara. When the time comes for his physical elements to disperse in death, he will give himself completely to the dispersal and die without regret or attachment. A person like that is *living* the truth of "samsara is nirvana" and is, at the same time, living and dying at will.

Here, I always urge people simply to live in the unborn Buddha-mind. I don't try to make anyone do anything else. We haven't any special rules. But since everyone got together and decided that they wanted to spend six hours each day (for a period of twelve sticks of incense) doing zazen, I let them do as they wish. That amount of time has been set aside for zazen. But the unborn Buddha-mind has no connection with those sticks of incense. It's just being at home in the Buddha-mind, not straying into illusion, and not seeking enlightenment beyond that. Just sit in the Buddha-mind, stand in the Buddha-mind, sleep in the Buddha-mind, awake in the Buddha-mind, do everything in the Buddha-mind—then you'll be functioning as a living Buddha in all that you do in your daily life. There's nothing further.

Now, in zazen, it's a matter of the Buddha-mind sitting at rest. It's the Buddha-mind doing continuous zazen. Zazen isn't limited to the time you sit. That's why, around here, if people have something to do while they're sitting, they're free to get up and do it. It's up to them, whatever they've a mind to do. Some of them will do *kinhin* for one stick of incense.[26] But they can't just continue walking, so then they sit down and for another stick of incense they do zazen. They can't be sleeping all the time, so they get up. They can't talk constantly, so they stop talking and do some zazen. They aren't bound by any set rules.

In recent times, wherever you go, you find that Zen teachers use "old tools" when they deal with pupils.[27] They seem to think they can't do the job without them. They're unable to teach directly, by thrusting themselves forward and confronting students without their tools. Those eyeless bonzes with their "tool Zen"—if they don't have their implements to help them, they aren't up to handling people.

What's worse, they tell practicers that unless they can raise a "great ball of doubt" and then break through it, there can't be any progress in Zen.[28] Instead of teaching them to live by the unborn Buddha-mind, they start by forcing them to raise this ball of doubt any way they can. People who don't have a doubt are now saddled with one. They've turned their Buddha-minds into "balls of doubt." It's absolutely wrong.

My religion has nothing to do with either "self-power" or "other-power."[29] It's beyond them both. My proof is this: While you face me and listen to me say this, if somewhere a sparrow chirps, or a crow caws, or a man or woman says something, or the wind rustles the leaves, though you sit there without any intent to listen, you will hear and distinguish each sound. Because it isn't yourself that's doing the listening, it isn't self-power. On the other hand, it wouldn't do you any good if you had someone else hear and distinguish the sounds for you. So it isn't other-power. That's the reason why I can say that my teaching has nothing to do with self-power or other-power and is beyond them both. When you're listening like this in the Unborn, each and every sound is heard as it occurs. And all other things as well, in just the same way, are perfectly well taken care of in the Unborn. Anyone who lives his life in the Unborn, whoever he may be, will find this to be true. No one who lives in the Unborn is concerned with self or other. He's beyond them both.

I went around the country wasting time and energy on ascetic practices, all because I wanted to discover my Buddha-mind. I ended up bringing on serious illness instead. I've been confined to sickbeds for long periods, so I've learned all about sickness at firsthand. Everyone who is born into this world and receives bodily form is therefore bound to experience illness. But if you become confirmed in the unborn Buddhamind, you aren't troubled by the suffering that normally accompanies illness. Illness and suffering are differentiated: The illness is illness, the suffering is suffering. Now, the way it works is this. Being originally unborn, the Buddha-mind has no concern with either pain or joy. Since being unborn means that it is completely detached from thought, and since it is through the arising of thoughts that you experience both pain and joy, so long as the Buddha-mind remains as it is in its original unbornness, unworried by and unattached to the illness, it doesn't experience suffering. But if a thought arises from the ground of the Unborn and you start to worry about your illness, you create suffering for yourself; you change your Buddha-mind into suffering. It can't be helped. The sufferings of hell itself are no different.

Now, suppose someone is suffering because he worries anxiously about his illness. The illness may at some point begin to improve, yet because he worries, over and above the original illness, about the medicine being wrong or about the physician being inept, he changes the Buddha-mind into various painful thoughts, until the disease in his mind becomes a more serious affliction than the original illness. While the turmoil of thoughts crowd through his mind as he attempts to escape from his illness, the original illness may gradually improve and he may regain his health. But now he suffers because he's plagued by the troubled thoughts churning in his mind, which have grown and intensified in the course of his illness and recovery.

But even though I say this, if someone who is down with an illness or undergoing any other kind of suffering were to say that he doesn't suffer, he would have to be called a liar. He's ignorant of the way in which the marvelous wisdom of the Buddha-mind works. If he pledged on his honor that he was positively not suffering, it would only mean that his suffering was taking the form of not suffering. There is no way such a person could be free from suffering. Since the working of illuminative wisdom is intrinsic to the Buddha-mind, by which it knows and perfectly differentiates not only suffering but all other things as well, when the sickness comes, the Buddha-mind remains free of any involvement or concern with pain or suffering. But, even then, since you will inevitably think about your sickness, it's best at such times to give yourself up to the sickness, and to moan when there is pain. Then, all the time, both when you're sick and when you're well, you'll be living in the unborn Buddha-mind. But you ought to be aware that when thought becomes involved in your suffering, the Buddha-mind is changed into the *thought* of sickness or the *thought* of suffering, quite apart from the sickness or suffering itself, and you will suffer because of that.

The unborn Buddha-mind is originally free from all thought. So long as a person is ignorant of the Buddha-mind's unbornness and suffers because he has changed it into thought, no matter how loudly he may deny his suffering, his denial—the notion that "I'm not suffering"—is only a determination he has created out of thought. He couldn't possibly be detached from suffering. He may think that he's not suffering, but inasmuch as he hasn't confirmed himself in the unborn Buddha-mind that is detached from birth and death, that very birth and death is the cause of his suffering.

The working of your bright, illuminating Buddha-mind is as different from an ordinary mirror as a cloud is from mud. Kyoto, Osaka, Edo, Sendai, Nagasaki, or wherever, once you've been and seen a place, even after many years pass and you're at an entirely different location, if someone else who has been there comes and talks to you about it, your conversation will go along in perfect agreement. Moreover, while a mirror is able only to illuminate and show objects a yard or two away at most, the working of the Buddha-mind's resplendent clarity is such that you can see and recognize a man over a block away; you can see a towering mountain peak fifty leagues distant, even behind rows of hills, and your Buddha-mind can tell that it's Mount Fuji, or Mount Kongō, or some other mountain. So while the Buddha-mind is often compared to a mirror, how vastly different its brightness really is! Even the sun and moon light up only the earth and the heavens. The marvelous brightness of the Buddha-mind, by means of words, is able to enlighten people and deliver them from their illusions one by one. And when someone hears these words, and understands and affirms them, he will know for himself that the Buddha-mind's wonderful brightness surpasses even the brightness of the sun and moon. What an incalculable treasure your Buddha-mind is!

A monk said to Bankei: I was born with a short temper. It's always flaring up. My master has remonstrated with me time and again, but that hasn't done any good. I know I should do something about it, but as I was born with a bad temper, I'm unable to rid myself of it no matter how hard I try. Is there anything I can do to correct it? This time, I'm hoping that with your teaching, I'll be able to cure myself. Then, when I go back home, I'll be able to face my master again, and of course I will benefit by it for the rest of my life. Please, tell me what to do.

Bankei: That's an interesting inheritance you have. Is your temper here now? Bring it out. I'll cure it for you.[30]

Monk: I'm not angry now. My temper comes on unexpectedly, when something provokes me.

Bankei: You weren't born with it then. You create it yourself when some pretext or other happens to appear. Where would your temper be at such times if you didn't cause it? You work yourself into a temper because of your partiality for yourself, opposing others in order to have your own way. Then you unjustly accuse your parents of having burdened you with a short temper. What an extremely unfilial son you are!

Each person receives the Buddha-mind from his parents when he's born. His illusion is something he produces all alone, by being partial to himself. It's foolish to think that it's inherent. When you don't produce your temper, where is it? All illusions are the same; as long as you don't produce them, they cease to exist. That's what everyone fails to realize. There they are, creating from their own selfish desires and deluded mental habits something that isn't inherent but thinking it is.

On account of this, they're unable to avoid being deluded in whatever they do.

You certainly must cherish your illusions dearly for you to change the Buddha-mind into them just so you can be deluded. If you only knew the great value of the Buddha-mind, there's no way you could ever be deluded again, not even if you wanted to be. Fix this clearly in your head: When you are not deluded, you are a Buddha, and that means you are enlightened. There is no other way for you to become a Buddha. So draw close and listen carefully and be sure that you understand what I say.

You create your outbursts of temper when the organs of your six senses [vision, hearing, smell, taste, touch, and faculty of mind] are stimulated by some external condition and incite you to oppose other people because you desire to assert your own preciously held ideas. When you have no attachment to self, there are no illusions. Have that perfectly clear.

All your parents gave you when you were born was a Buddha-mind. Nothing else. What have you done with it? From the time you were a tiny baby, you've watched and listened to people losing their tempers around you. You've been schooled in this, until you too have become habituated to irascibility. So now you indulge in frequent fits of anger. But it's foolish to think that's inherent. Right now, if you realize you've been mistaken and don't allow your temper to arise anymore, you'll have no temper to worry about. Instead of trying to correct it, don't produce it in the first place. That's the quickest way, don't you agree? Trying to do something about it after it occurs is very troublesome and futile besides. Don't get angry to begin with, then there's no need to cure anything. There's nothing left to cure.

Once you've realized this and you stop creating that temper of yours, you'll find that you won't have any other illusions either, not even if you want to, for you'll be living constantly in the unborn Buddha-mind. There is nothing else.

Since everything is in perfect harmony if you live and work in the unborn mind of the Buddhas, my school is also known as the "Buddha-mind" sect. Live in the Buddha-mind and you're a living Buddha from that moment on. This is the priceless thing "directly pointed to."[31] I want you to trust completely in what I've been telling you. Do just as I've said. To start with, try to stay in the Unborn for thirty days. Once you've accustomed yourself to that, then you'll find it's impossible to live apart from the Unborn. It will come naturally to you then, and even if you don't want to, even if you grow tired of it, there'll still be no way you can avoid living in the Unborn and doing an admirable job of it too. Everything you do will be according to the Unborn. You'll be a living Buddha.

You should all listen to my words as if you were newly born this very day. If something's on your mind, if you have any preconception, you can't really take in what I say. But if you listen as if you were a newborn child, it'll be like hearing me for the first time. Since then there's nothing in your mind, you can take it right in, grasp it even from a single word, and fully realize the Buddha's Dharma.

A laywoman from Izumo, who had come to the retreat because she had heard of Bankei and his teaching, asked: According to what you say, all we have to do is simply remain effortlessly in the Buddha-mind. Don't you think that teaching is too lightweight?

Bankei: Lightweight? You set no store by the Buddha-mind. You get angry and turn it into a fighting spirit. You give vent to selfish desires and change it into a hungry ghost or do something foolish and convert it into an animal. You deludedly turn the Buddha-mind into all sorts of different things—that's lightweight, not my teaching. Nothing is of more gravity, and nothing more praiseworthy, than living in the Buddha-mind. So you may think when I tell you to live in the Buddha-mind that it is lightweight, but believe me, it's just because it has such weight that you are unable to do it.

This, however, might give you the idea that living in the Buddha-mind is a very difficult business. But isn't it true that if you listen carefully to my teaching, understand it well, and live in the Buddha-mind, then, simply and easily, without doing any hard work, you're a living Buddha this very day?

You decided after hearing what I said that dwelling effortlessly in the Buddha-mind was an easy matter. But in fact it's not easy, so you go on transforming it into a fighting spirit, a hungry ghost, or an animal. You get angry, even over trifles. When you do, you create the cause of rebirth as a fighting spirit. So though you may not be aware of it, you're spending your existence as a human being creating a fighting spirit of the first order. And sure enough, if you work earnestly at it, you'll not only be a fighting spirit during your lifetime, you'll fall into such an existence after you die as well, have no doubt about it.

On account of self-interest, you toil away to turn the Buddha-mind into greed and desire. Since that's the cause of rebirth as a denizen of the realm of hungry ghosts, you're unknowingly paving the way for rebirth into that realm. You're readying yourself for a postmortem fall into a hungry ghost existence. It's a foregone conclusion; you'll surely end up there.

Owing to selfish thoughts and aims, you dwell on one thought after another, fretting senselessly over things that can get you nowhere. Continuing on like that, unable to stop, you turn the Buddha-mind into ignorance. Ignorance causes you to be reborn as an animal. It's clear even now while you're alive and busily creating the cause of such a wretched fate that when you die you'll enter that existence.

I see people unaware of this, dedicating their lives to carefully fashioning the very causes of their rebirth into the three evil realms.[32] It's pitiful. They're reserving seats for the passage. But when you don't change your Buddha-mind into a fighting spirit, hungry ghost, or animal, you can't avoid dwelling naturally in the Buddha-mind. It's obvious, isn't it?

The laywoman: Yes, of course. It's true! I have no words to thank you.

A monk: You're always teaching people that they should live in the Unborn. To me that seems like telling them to live purposelessly, without any aim.

Bankei: You call dwelling in the unborn Buddha-mind being without purpose? You don't stay in the unborn Buddha-mind yourself. Instead, you're always working enthusiastically at other things, doing this, doing that, spending all your time transforming your Buddha-mind into something else. What could be more purposeless than that?

The monk made no reply.

Bankei: Live in the Unborn. It's certainly not purposeless.

A monk: To live in the Buddha-mind as you say would mean to live in a state of unknowing, to be insensible.

Bankei: What if someone came up behind you without your knowing it and suddenly poked you in the back with a gimlet? Would you feel pain?

The monk: Of course I would.

Bankei: Then you're not unknowing or insensible, are you? If you were, it wouldn't hurt. You feel it because you're not insensible, and you never have been. Have confidence in me. Live in the unborn Buddha-mind.

A monk: You tell people to dwell in the Unborn, but it seems to me that would mean remaining totally indifferent to things.[33]

Bankei: While you face me there listening innocently to what I say, suppose someone should come up behind you and touch a firebrand to your back. Would it feel hot?

The monk: Of course it would.

Bankei: In that case, you aren't indifferent. How could someone who feels heat be indifferent? You feel it because you aren't indifferent. You have no difficulty telling what is hot and what is cold, without having to give rise to a thought to make such a distinction. The very fact that you ask that question about being indifferent or not shows that you're not indifferent. You have no trouble telling by yourself whether you're indifferent or not—that's because you're not indifferent. So you see, the Buddha-mind with its illuminating wisdom is capable of discriminating things with a miraculous efficiency. It is anything but indifferent. How could any human being, who is able to think, be indifferent? A man who was really indifferent wouldn't be engaged in thinking. I can assure you that you are not indifferent and that you never have been.

A monk: I don't know why it is, but my mind often seems to be somewhere else. Could you help me to keep my mind from playing truant like that?

Bankei: The unborn mind of the Buddhas that all people receive from their parents when they're born is wonderfully bright and illuminating. No one—and that includes all of you—is ever separated from it. This absentmindedness of yours is the same. Your mind's not really somewhere else. It's only that you haven't learned about the Buddha-mind, so instead of just dwelling in it, you change it into various other things. Then even though you listen to things, you can't really take them in—you don't really hear them. You're not absentminded, what you're doing is making the Buddha-mind into these other things.

Would someone whose mind is really somewhere else be inquiring whether it was or not? If your mind were somewhere else, you would hardly be aware of it. You wouldn't be asking questions about it. You're not even away from it when you sleep, because if someone calls to you and tells you to wake up, you will respond to him and wake right up. You've never been apart from your mind in the past, you won't be apart from it in the future, and you're not apart from it right now. None of you here has ever been separated from your mind, just as none of you is an unenlightened person. You've each been born with the Buddha-mind. It's your birthright.

After you leave here today, be toward all things just as you are right at this moment as you listen to me speak, and you'll be in the unborn Buddha-mind. People form bad habits, strive for personal gain, and fall into illusion, all on account of the defilements produced from their desires and passions. Leaving the Buddha-mind, they become unenlightened. But originally there are no unenlightened people.

Suppose two men are walking together down the same path. One steals things, the other doesn't. Although the one who steals is no less a human being than his companion, he's branded with a special name: *thief*. He has to carry that name around with him wherever he goes. But no one calls the other man a thief, and he doesn't have to be burdened with that name. The thief is like an unenlightened man, a deluded human being, and the one who doesn't steal and isn't deluded is like a man of the Unborn who lives in the Buddha-mind.

No mother ever gave birth to a thief. The truth of the matter is this. From the time the thief is a small child, he begins to be habituated unwittingly to the wrong inclinations, taking what belongs to other people. Little by little, as he grows to manhood, his selfishness comes more and more to the fore, until he learns to be a skillful thief and is unable to keep his hands off others' property. Now, if he didn't steal to begin with, he'd have no need to stop. But he doesn't make the slightest mention of his own failing. He claims that his inclination to steal others' property is something he can't stop because he's a *born thief*. That's ridiculous. The proof that a mother doesn't bear children to be thieves is that there are no congenital thieves. People turn into thieves by watching others exercising their bad habits and imitating them, stealing things of their own accord, because of their own greed. Now, how can that be called inborn?

A thief may rationalize his problem by laying the blame on his karma, telling you that he can't help himself; he's unable to keep from stealing because of his bad karma. There's not a word about the selfish desires that have fixed this reprehensible habit deeply in his character over a long period of time. It's a lot of nonsense. You don't steal because of karma. Stealing itself is the karma. Supposing theft were caused by karma, supposing stealing were inborn, it's still possible for a thief to realize that what he's been doing is wrong and to stop stealing. So it's not true that he can't stop. There's not even any reason for him to stop, if he doesn't steal to begin with.

Even the greatest scoundrel who ever lived, a man who until just yesterday may have been the object of everyone's contemptuous pointing and whispering, if he realizes today that what he's been doing is wrong and starts to live in his Buddha-mind, that man is a living Buddha from then on.

When I was a youth, we had a rascal in this neighborhood called the "Kappa."[34] He was a notorious robber in the mold of Kumasaka Chōhan.[35] He plied his trade on the highways. He had acquired an uncanny knack of being able to tell at a glance just how much money a person had with him. He was always right. It was amazing. Anyway, he was eventually caught and thrown into Osaka prison. After a long period locked up in a cell, because he was such a master thief, his death sentence was finally lifted and he was released, on the condition that he work as an agent for the constabulary.[36] He later became a sculptor of Buddhist images, living in Osaka, and made a name for himself as a master sculptor. He ended his days as a practicer of the Pure Land faith and passed away peacefully in a Nembutsu samadhi.[37]

By mending his ways, even a notorious thief like the Kappa died with a deep aspiration for rebirth in the Pure Land. So where is a man who steals because of the depth of his karma or the blackness of his sins? Robbery's the bad karma. Robbery's the sin. If you don't steal, you don't have the karma or the sin. Whether you steal or not is determined by you yourself, not by any karma.

And don't think that what I've been saying applies only to stealing. It's just as true of any human illusions. They're all the same. Having illusions or not having them depends upon your own mind and nothing else. If you have illusions, you're an unenlightened person; if you don't, you're a Buddha. Outside of this, there's no shortcut to being a Buddha. Each one of you should fix this unshakably in your mind.

A layman: Everyone says that you're able to read others' minds. Is it true?[38]

Bankei: There's no place in my school for strange things like that. Even if I did have such an ability, because of the unbornness of the Buddha-mind, I wouldn't use it. People get the idea that I can read minds from hearing me comment on the concerns of those who come to see me. I can't read minds. I'm no different from any of you. When you dwell in the Buddha-mind, which is the very source of all the Buddha's supernatural powers, everything is resolved and in perfect harmony without recourse to such powers. So I don't need to get involved in a lot of side issues. All the true unborn Dharma needs to do the job is direct personal comments on you and your lives.

A layman: I've practiced diligently for a long time, but even when I think I've advanced to where I won't backslide anymore, there's still a strong tendency to do so, and I sometimes slip back. How can I become so that I won't backslide?

Bankei: Live in the unborn Buddha-mind. Then there's no regression. No need for advancement. Any idea of wanting to make progress is already a regression from the place of the Unborn. A man of the Unborn has nothing to do with either advancing or backsliding. He's always beyond them both.

A monk: I've been working on "Hyakujō's Fox" for a long time.[39] I've concentrated on it as hard as I know how, but I still can't seem to grasp it. I think it's because I'm unable to achieve total concentration. If possible, I would like to receive your teaching.

Bankei: I don't make people here waste their time on worthless old documents like that. You don't know yet about your unborn Buddha-mind and its illuminative wisdom, so I'll tell you about it. That will take care of everything. Pay careful attention.

Bankei then taught him about the Unborn. The monk was completely convinced. He is said to have developed into an exceptional priest.

Another monk (who had been listening to this): If that's true, what about all the old koans? Are they useless and unnecessary?

Bankei: When worthy Zen masters of the past dealt with those who came to them, every word and every movement were appropriate to the moment. It was a matter of responding to their students and their questions face-to-face. They had no other purpose in mind. Now, there's no way for me to tell you whether that was necessary, or helpful, or not. If everyone just stays in the Buddha-mind, that's all he has to do—that takes care of everything. Why do you want to go and think up other things to do? There's no need to. Just dwell in the Unborn. You're eager to make this extra work for yourself—but all you're doing is creating illusion. Stop doing that. Stay in the Unborn. The Unborn and its marvelous illumination are perfectly realized in the Buddha-mind.

A priest said: Suppose right now a triple invalid [a man at once blind, deaf, and mute] appeared before you.[40] How would you deal with him?

Bankei: You must think very highly of these triple invalids, the way you spend so much time studying about them, trying eagerly to join their ranks. But right at this moment, you are not a triple invalid. Instead of trying to become one—which would be very difficult anyhow—you should get to the bottom of your own self. That's the first order of business for you, since you don't have any of those disabilities your-self. Going around talking about all these other things will get you nowhere. Pay attention now to what I'm going to tell you.

Bankei always had a subtemple set aside for the priests of the Precepts sect who came for the summer retreats to study with him.[41] At the great winter retreat, there was a contingent of as many as fifty-three priests of that denomination in attendance. Two among them asked Bankei: We observe all the 250 Buddhist precepts. We believe that will enable us to attain Buddhahood. Would you say that is good or bad?

Bankei: There's nothing in the least wrong with it. It's a good thing. But you can't say it's the best. It's shameful to wear your rules as a badge and call yourselves the "Precepts" sect, as if you think that's somehow superior. Basically, precepts are something initiated by the Buddha because of evil priests who transgressed against the Dharma. The 250 precepts enumerate the different kinds of offenses committed by disreputable priests. Priests of the true stripe never take it upon themselves to uphold precepts so that they won't violate the Dharma's conventions. For a person who doesn't drink, there's no need for precepts against alcohol. Those who don't steal don't need precepts against theft. Precepts against lying are wasted on a truthful man. You tell me that you observe the precepts, but to observe them or violate them is actually something which should be of concern only to an evil priest. When you start saying, "We're the Precepts sect," and set up precepts as superior, you're advertising yourselves as evil priests. Why, it's like a person parading as an evil man, imitating him, even though he's a good man. Wouldn't you think that reproachable?

The Unborn is the mind of the Buddhas. If you live according to it, then from the first there's no distinction between observing and not observing. Those are designations that arise after the fact. They're one or more removes from the place of the Unborn.

The two priests thus gained a deep understanding of Bankei's teaching. Before they left, they thanked him profusely and told him that they realized completely the truth of his words.

During the retreat, a large number of women from the provinces of Tamba, Tango, Izumo, and Mino came to see Bankei. Some were mourning the death of a parent. Others were grieving inconsolably for the loss of a child. They came hoping to lessen the pain of their bereavement by meeting with Bankei. He spoke to them:

The sorrow of a parent who loses his child, of a child who loses his father or his mother, is the same the world over. The karma that binds together parent and child is deep. When death takes one from the other, sorrow is only natural. And yet the dead won't come back, no matter how great your sorrow may be. Should you spend your lives in unbroken sadness, grieving misguidedly over something you can't possibly change? Have you ever heard of anyone who was successful in restoring the dead to life because of the intensity of his sorrow? Of course you haven't. And since there's no way for the dead to return, don't spend any more time on your grief. Stop mourning right now. Use the time instead to do some zazen, recite a sutra, or offer some flowers and incense for the dead person. That will be a real demonstration of your filial devotion or parental love.

Now, you don't know it, but by grieving like this, you're ac-

tually causing trouble for the dead person. You all mourn
your parents or children because you feel sorry for them. You
believe that you're doing it for their sakes. But you're really
hurting them. For all your professions of pity, you're not acting as if you pitied them at all; you're acting as if you had
something against them. Well, if you do, then lamenting them
is the right way to express it. But if you feel truly sorry for
them, you should stop mourning. It's wrong to mourn them
out of pity. You could do nothing more foolish than to go on
like this, marching your minds around your grief day and
night, lamenting the unchangeable, filling every thought with
sadness and regret, uselessly pouring out endless tears, ruin-
ing your health in the process, oblivious to what others try to
tell you. It's senseless. And don't forget, folly or ignorance is
the cause of an animal existence. Were you to die in such a
state of mind, it goes without saying that you'd fall together
with your parent or child, right into an animal existence. If
that happened, you'd have to spend that entire existence constantly fighting with each other.

Each person comes into the world with nothing but the
Buddha-mind his parents give him. When you turn this unborn Buddha-mind into a state of ignorance because of your
parent or child, inwardly you're living as a first-rate animal.
This is true during your lifetime, but even after you die, you'll
fall directly into an animal existence, where parent and child
are doomed constantly to fight each other tooth and nail.
Now, do you see anything praiseworthy in that? I'm sure you'll
agree that it's absurd and deplorable beyond words.

Pay attention, then. It's natural for parents to feel compassion for their children and for children to be devoted to their
parents, but if the child saddens his parents by dying first, and
causes them to mourn and become ignorant beasts as a result,
can you call that filial piety? Do you imagine that an unfilial

child who dies, causing his parents to fall into an animal existence, is destined for a peaceful life in his future existence? Of
course not. The outcome can be only one: Parent and child
will fall together into the evil paths of existence.

If the parent allows himself to be overwhelmed by grieving
over what cannot be otherwise, and becomes deluded on account of his child, turning into an animal himself and sending
the child he deeply loves into hell as well, can that be called
parental love? It would be parental hate. By the same token, a
child who turns his father and mother into animals because of
his death is deeply unfilial. The parents, led by their child into
turning their Buddha-minds into animals, go to hell along
with him, where all three of them become denizens of that
wretchedness and fight one another as deadly enemies.

You can see, then, that even if your child or parent is taken
from you, if you go on grieving endlessly, the only thing you'll
accomplish is to condemn him or her to great misery. You
won't be able to mourn now without being reminded that
you are thereby causing harm. Or could you mourn even
then? I don't think so. So recite a sutra instead, or do zazen,
or offer some flowers or incense for the sake of his or her future existence. That will demonstrate your sense of pity and
compassion far better. It may even happen that a person who
isn't religiously minded to begin with will, upon suffering the
loss of a loved one, acquire true faith and the desire for birth
in a favorable future existence. If so, he can be said to have
been saved by the deceased, since the faith he acquired stems
from the bereavement. If a child's death can turn his parent to
religion, it can be said to have a redeeming merit. He'll be doing something for his parent far greater than anything he did
while he was alive.

Do you think that after saving his parent with this act of
deep filial piety an unwelcome destination awaits the child in

his next existence? No. Both parent and child are thus saved. If the parent becomes a person of faith owing to his child and lives in the unborn Buddha-mind, even the child's death has a redeeming aspect. The child performs the role of a good religious teacher to his parent.[42]

It's commendable that you've all come such long distances at this cold season of the year simply to meet me and try to ease the sorrow in your hearts. If you want to make your long journeys truly worthwhile, the thing for you to do is to return to your homes. Since you've come here for the purpose of seeing me and dispelling some of the grief you feel, don't take your sorrow back with you. Leave it here with me, and go home without it. If you can grasp thoroughly what I've said, I don't think that you'll indulge in any more grief, knowing that it only works to the disadvantage of you and your loved ones.

If someone finds, even then, that she can't stop grieving, she should remember that she's changing her Buddha-mind into ignorance. If she's a child, she'll fall into hell for the sin of transforming her parents into a state of ignorance; if she's a parent, she'll fall into an animal existence hand in hand with her child for having turned her Buddha-mind into ignorance on her child's account. Were someone to tell you that it's right for you to grieve and lament, it's advice you should never listen to. Or would you grieve, even at such cost?

Thereupon, the women who had come to Bankei with grief-sick hearts declared as a group: We understand all that you have told us. You have cleared the anguish and sorrow from our minds. We are deeply grateful. We cannot thank you enough.

Bankei: Good! I want you to remain just the way you are now, even after you've left the temple and are back in your own homes.

The women: We wept because we felt so deeply about our loved ones. But what you've told us has convinced us. Mourning them only brings harm to them. We don't want to do anything to hurt them. In our ignorance, we didn't realize what we were doing. From now on, even after we return home, we will always remain in the Unborn and never change our Buddha-minds into anything else. We shall never mourn them again, even if someone should encourage us to.

The main figure of worship at the Ryūmon-ji was an image of the bodhisattva Kannon carved by Bankei.[43] Aware of this, a monk from Ōshū, in northern Japan, who was standing against a pillar, asked in the middle of one of Bankei's talks: Is that figure a new Buddha or an old one?

Bankei: What does it look like to you?

The monk: A new Buddha.

Bankei: If it looks to you like a new Buddha, then that's what it is, and that's the end of it. Why did you have to ask me? Since you don't know yet that the Unborn is the Buddha-mind, you ask useless questions like that, thinking it's Zen. Instead of bothering everyone here with foolish questions, sit down, keep your mouth shut for a while, and listen carefully to what I say.

A monk: When I fall into a deep sleep, sometimes I dream. Why do we have dreams? What do they mean?

Bankei: If you're sound asleep, you don't dream. Your dreams mean that you're not sound asleep.

The monk had no reply.

A layman from Izumo Province bowed before Bankei and asked: Is it true that when someone is enlightened as you are, he can really see the past, present, and future worlds just as if he is looking at the palm of his hand?[44]

Bankei looked at him and said: Is that question something you thought up beforehand? Or did it occur to you just now?

The layman: It didn't come into my head just now when I asked it. It's something I thought about before.

Bankei: In that case, it will be all right to leave that for later. First of all, what you must do right now is to find out about yourself. Until you've completed that, no matter how much I described to you what the three worlds looked like, you wouldn't be able to understand what I was saying, because you couldn't see them for yourself. Once you've found out about yourself, the question of both seeing the three worlds and not seeing them will be something you'll know about quite naturally. There's no sense in my trying to tell you about it and no need in your asking me. Rather than do what you should be doing today, dealing with the matter of your self, you come here with worthless questions that you don't really need to know about now, and miss the point completely; you're misdirecting your effort to what's altogether irrelevant to you. It's like counting up someone else's money for him, when you're not going to get a penny of it yourself! So listen to what I'm going to tell you. The important thing for you to do is to find out all about your self. Pay careful attention to my instructions. If you follow them, and become absolutely sure of them yourself, that very instant you're a living Buddha. Then you'll realize how mistaken you've been to carry around needless questions such as the one you just asked, and you won't direct your effort where you shouldn't.

A monk had practiced zazen assiduously for twenty years, even grudging time to lie down for sleep. He spared no effort and tried various methods to achieve enlightenment, but all without success. Then, chancing to hear reports of Bankei and his teaching, he came to meet the master. Bankei promptly gave him his teaching of the Unborn. The monk listened and was immediately convinced: There's never been a teaching like this before. Now I see I've been wrong all these years.

Bankei: Even twenty years of hard practice can't equal the single word "Unborn" that I spoke today.

The monk: Yes, you're right. It's just as you say.

THE HŌSHIN-JI SERMONS

Toward the end of autumn in the third year of Genroku (1690), Bankei crossed the Inland Sea to Marugame, in Sanuki Province, and delivered talks at the Hōshin-ji.[45]

The twenty-third day of the eighth month—
the midday sermon

What I teach everyone in these talks of mine is the unborn Buddha-mind of illuminative wisdom, nothing else. Everyone is endowed with this Buddha-mind, only he doesn't know it. My reason for coming and speaking to you like this is to make it known to you.

Well then, what does it mean, you're endowed with a Buddha-mind? Each of you now present decided to come here from your home in the desire to hear what I have to say. Now, if a dog barked beyond the temple walls while you're listening to me, you'd hear it and know it was a dog barking. If a crow cawed, you'd hear it and know it was a crow. You'd hear an adult's voice as an adult's and a child's as a child's.

You didn't come here in order to hear a dog bark, a crow caw, or any of the other sounds that might come from outside the temple during my talk. Yet while you're here, you'd hear those sounds. Your eyes see and distinguish reds and whites and other colors, and your nose can tell good smells from bad. You could have had no way of knowing beforehand of any of the sights, sounds, or smells you might encounter at this meeting, yet you're able nevertheless to recognize these unforeseen sights and sounds as you encounter them, without premeditation. That's because you're seeing and hearing in the Unborn.

That you do see and hear and smell in this way without giving rise to the *thought* that you will is the proof that this inherent Buddha-mind is unborn and possessed of a wonderful illuminative wisdom. The Unborn manifests itself in the thought "I want to see" or "I want to hear" not being born. When a dog howls, even if ten million people said in chorus that it was the sound of a crow cawing, I doubt if you'd be convinced. It's highly unlikely there would be any way they could delude you into believing what they said. That's owing to the marvelous awareness and unbornness of your Buddha-mind. The reason I say it's in the "Unborn" that you see and hear in this way is because the mind doesn't give "birth" to any thought or inclination to see or hear. Therefore it is *unborn*. Being unborn, it's also undying: It's not possible for what is not born to perish. This is the sense in which I say that all people have an unborn Buddha-mind.

Each and every Buddha and bodhisattva in the universe, and everyone in this world of humans as well, has been endowed with it. But being ignorant of the fact that you have a Buddha-mind, you live in illusion. Why is it you're deluded? Because you're partial to yourself. What does that mean? Well, let's take something close to home. Suppose you heard that your next-door neighbor was whispering bad things about you. You'd get angry. Every time you saw his face, you'd immediately feel indignant. You'd think, Oh, what an unreasonable, hateful person! And everything he said would appear to you in a bad light. All because you're wedded to your self. By becoming angry, losing your temper, you just transform your one Buddha-mind into the sinful existence of the fighting spirits.

If your neighbor praised you instead, or said something that pleased you, you'd be immediately delighted, even if the praise was totally undeserved and the pleasure you felt unfounded, a product of your wishful thinking. The delight you experience when this happens is due to that same obstinate, constitutional preference to yourself.

Just stop and look back to the origin of this self of yours. When you were born, your parents didn't give you any happy, evil, or bitter thoughts. There was only your Buddha-mind. Afterward, when your intelligence appeared, you saw and heard other people saying and doing bad things, and you learned them and made them yours. By the time you reached adulthood, deep-seated habits, formed in this way of your own manufacture, had emerged. Now, cherishing yourself and your own ideas, you turn your Buddha-mind into the path of fighting spirits. If you covet what belongs to other people, kindling selfish desires for something that can never be yours, you create the path of hungry ghosts, and you change the Buddha-mind into that kind of existence. This is what is known as transmigration.

If you realize fully the meaning of what I've just said, and do not lose your temper, or think you must have this, or decide that you don't like that, or have feelings of bitterness or pity—that in itself is the unborn Buddha-mind. You'll be a living Buddha.

It's the same thing I always tell everyone about the Buddha-mind. I do it because when I was a young boy I tried very hard to attain the Buddha-mind myself. In the course of my practice, I sought help from Buddhist teachers. I had interviews with them and questioned them about the various doubts and uncertainties that arose in me. But nobody could give me any help. So I went on practicing very hard. I did zazen. I went and lived in the mountains. I disciplined myself as severely as I possibly could. But none of it helped a bit. I didn't get any closer to understanding the Buddha-mind.

Finally, when I was twenty-six years old, it suddenly came to me, and I arrived at my realization. I've been telling others about the unborn Buddha-mind ever since. I'm sure there's no one else who can teach these things as thoroughly as I do.

You can gather from what I've told you that my practice lasted many long years and that I came to realize my Buddha-mind only after great hardship. But you can grasp your Buddha-minds very easily, right where you sit, without that long, punishing practice. That shows the relation that links you to Buddhahood is stronger than mine was. You're all very fortunate indeed.

Ever since I realized the wonderful working of the Buddha-mind, I've been going around telling people about it. Many of them have become convinced of it too. Of course, it's not something I learned from a Buddhist teacher; I discovered it on my own. And since I did, each time I tell others about it at these meetings, my words come from personal knowledge and experience. Hearing about it only once or twice probably won't be enough, so you should listen as many times as you need to. If you have any questions about it, ask them, and I'll answer them for you.

I was once asked some questions by a Confucian scholar in Edo. I think it would do you good to hear about them. He said: "I have no trouble accepting what you say about 'unborn, undying.' It's quite reasonable. While the body is strong, it's true that the ears hear sounds, the eyes see and distinguish things, the nose recognizes smells, the mouth perceives the tastes of the five flavors and speaks, all in the absence of any conscious thought to do so. But once the body dies, no matter how much it's spoken to, it can make no response; it can't tell one color from another, and it's ignorant of all smells. You can't very well speak of either unborn or undying then."

Now, the thrust of this argument, while it may seem quite plausible, is wrong. But we can use it to make the principle of "unborn, undying" better understood. Since the physical body is something that was born and is composed of the elements of earth, water, fire, and air brought temporarily together, according to the principle that what is born cannot avoid perishing, it, too, must one day perish.[46] But the Buddha-mind is unborn; the body may be burned with fire or decompose through interment, but the Buddha-mind cannot. The unborn Buddha-mind simply makes the born body its temporary home. While it resides there, it is free to hear, see, smell, and so forth. But when the body perishes and it loses its dwelling place, it can no longer do those things. It's as simple as that. The body, being created, has a birth and a death, but the mind, which is originally the unborn Buddha-mind, does not. It stands to reason, doesn't it? It's the same as Shakamuni's death or nirvana: *ne* is the unborn, and *han* is the undying mind.[47] Both point to the Unborn.

Listen closely, because whatever I say, it's always about your inherent Buddha-mind. The important thing for you is to clarify it for yourself.

Basically, there's not a thing wrong with you; it's only that you let slight, inadvertent mistakes change the Buddha-mind into thought. A thief, for example, begins by pilfering only trifles. He finds it a wonderfully convenient way of acquiring things. It doesn't even require any capital. And so he advances beyond petty theft and becomes a highly accomplished robber. But finally, it becomes impossible to keep from being found out. He's discovered, arrested, trussed up, and dealt with by the law. When this happens, and he's brought out for punishment, he often forgets all about the offenses he has committed and becomes indignant and resentful toward the blameless officers of the law, reproaching them bitterly for being so hard on him. I'm sure you'll agree that he's greatly mistaken. What he has done is to turn his valuable Buddha-mind into the way of hungry ghosts or animals because of a small mistake.

I have a hermitage at Yamashina near Kyoto.[48] When I stay there, I go into Kyoto every day, passing by way of the Awataguchi, where the prison is. There, severed heads are set out on pikes, and crucified criminals are displayed before the prison gates. Since I pass by there quite frequently, I often come upon such sights.[49]

In Edo, there was a criminal prosecutor for the shogunate named Koide Ōsumi, with whom I was well acquainted. Whenever I visited him at his residence, criminals of various sorts would be brought before his magistrates for beatings and other punishments. They suffered miserably. But when this happened, they forgot all about their guilt and showed deep resentment toward the officers administering the punishment, as if their misery were somehow the fault of the officers. Later, I used to visit on the days of general abstinence set aside by the shogunate, when the criminals weren't brought for punishment.[50] But they are a good example of what can happen from a seemingly minor mistake. Let it be a lesson to encourage you to remain directly in the Buddha-mind you were born with and to stay clear of illusion, partialness, and selfish desires. They're the source of all the bad habits that insinuate themselves into your character.

The first requirement for anyone who works as a servant, man or woman, is single-minded devotion. There should be no thought at all for yourself; everything you do is for your master's sake. This exercise of total loyalty to your master is at the same time filial devotion to your parents. Should you do something wrong or harmful to your master's interests because of a self-interest you weren't born with and fail in your responsibility to him, you turn the Buddha-mind that you were born with into an evil thing and into the bargain are being very unfilial to your father and mother. If, on the other hand, you are a dutiful son or daughter, your devotion to your parents will be felt by your master, whose kindness toward you will then increase. When your parents learn of this kindness, they can't help being greatly pleased. In such a case, loyalty to your master is simultaneously filial piety, and filial piety is devotion to your master. This shows how essential it is for you to have a firm understanding of the unborn Buddha-mind.

When your mother bears you, you have neither bad habits of behavior nor selfish desires of any kind; your mind has no inclination to favor yourself. There's nothing but the Buddha-mind. But from the age of about four or five, you begin to learn all manner of wrong behavior by watching the people around you, and by listening you learn from them their ill-favored knowledge. Making your way through life under such conditions, it's little wonder that selfish desires emerge, leading to a strong self-partiality, which is the source of all your illusions and evil acts. If this self-partiality ceases to exist, illusion doesn't occur. That place of nonoccurrence is where you reside when you live in the Unborn. Buddhahood and the Buddha-mind are found nowhere else.

So if there is any doubt in anyone's mind about the principle of this, I want you to ask me about it, whatever it is. Have no hesitation whatever. That's what I'm here for. This isn't like inquiring about something of passing importance in your worldly life; it's a question that involves the future existence extending endlessly before you. If you have any doubts or questions, you should ask them now. Since it's not certain when I'll be able to meet with you again, I urge you to take advantage of this opportunity to clear up anything you have trouble with. If you can come to complete understanding of the unborn nature of your Buddha-mind, it will be to your great and lasting benefit.

The twenty-fifth day of the eighth month—
the morning sermon

You all assembled here before daybreak to listen to what I have to say. I'm going to tell you about the Buddha-mind, the mind of the Unborn. You've come here this early in the morning because you expected to hear something out of the ordinary. You wouldn't be here if you didn't.

Those of you who have reached the age of fifty have lived your fifty years totally unaware that you've had a Buddha-mind. If you're thirty, you've been ignorant of your Buddha-mind for thirty years, right up to this morning. You've all been slumbering the years away. But today at this gathering, if you come to understand thoroughly that you have an unborn Buddha-mind and go on to live in the Unborn, at that moment you become a living Buddha for countless future ages.

My only reason for speaking to people like this is because I want to make everyone know about the marvelously illuminating clarity of the unborn Buddha-mind. When you've confirmed it for yourself, you're the Buddha-mind from then on. No different from Shakamuni himself. The Buddha-body is yours once and for all, for endless ages, and you won't ever fall into the evil ways again.

And yet, should you grasp the unborn Buddha-mind at this meeting and then return home and let yourself be upset over something you see or hear, even if it's a trifling thing, that little bit of anger will make the unborn mind, to which you were just enlightened, change into the way of the fighting spirits or hungry ghosts, increasing the great evil of the life you lived prior to hearing about the Unborn by hundreds of millions of times and causing you to pass endlessly through the wheel of existence.

I'm sure not a single person among you would tell me that he was averse to becoming a Buddha. That's the reason I try to tell everyone I can about my teaching. Once they're able to understand it, they're living Buddhas from then on.

Now, what if I were to tell you that you didn't have to become Buddhas? Suppose I tried to urge you to go to hell instead? I don't think I'd see many of you volunteering to make the trip. The fact that you're here at this meeting to listen to my talk is proof of that. You left your warm beds before dawn to come here, and now you sit there packed in together without a complaint, because your minds are set on becoming Buddhas. Inasmuch as you have come, you must be very careful from now on to remain in the Buddha-mind in whatever you do.

Why do you think we've been born into the human world? We've received our present mind and body in order to become Buddhas.[51] In my own case, the desire to become a

Buddha was something I had my mind set on from the time I was a small boy. I worked very hard at it for a long time. I was able to become a Buddha. Now, unless you become Buddhas in your present lives, you'll fall into the realms of the hungry ghosts or animals. Once you've fallen into an animal existence, it will be hard for you ever to become Buddhas, not even in hundreds of millions of ages. It's easy to see why. You could lead a cow or horse in front of me here, and I could give it the same teaching that I give you. But would the animal understand it? Of course not. Once you've become an animal, it's too late. You can't understand then about things like Buddha or Dharma. It transmigrated and came to this sorry pass because in its previous existence the aspiration to become a Buddha didn't arise. Now that each of you has heard about how the Buddha-mind works, you should start being unborn today and that way avoid transmigrating. It all depends on your own mind.

Now, you're probably all wondering what this unborn Buddha-mind is like. Well, while you're sitting there facing me and trying to catch what it is I'm saying, if the bark of a dog or the cry of a street vendor should find its way in here from outside the temple walls, though you're listening to me, each of you would hear it, even though you had no intention to do so, thanks to the working of the Buddha-mind, which hears and understands in the Unborn. The Buddha-mind, unborn and illuminating all things with perfect clarity, is like a mirror, standing clear and spotlessly polished. A mirror, as you know, reflects anything that's before it. Whatever's placed in front of it never fails to be reflected, though the mirror has no idea or intention of doing so. And when the object is taken away, the mirror doesn't reflect it any longer, though it makes no decision to cease reflecting. Now, that's just how the unborn

Buddha-mind works. You see and hear all things, no matter what they are, although you haven't generated a single thought to see or hear them, because of the vital working of the unborn Buddha-mind each of you received at birth.

I go on explaining things to you like this to make you understand. If you can't grasp it today, then I don't suppose you could understand it no matter how many times you listened to me. But those who do understand about their unborn Buddha-mind, after only this one meeting—those people are living Buddhas now and for endless future ages.

Let me give you an example. Suppose you didn't know how to get from Edo to Kyoto, and you asked the way from someone who did. You would fix well in your mind all the details of the directions he gave you. If you followed them exactly, you wouldn't have any trouble reaching your destination. Today, in the same way, if you listen carefully to what I tell you and then arrive at an understanding of it, you're living in the Buddha-mind right then and there. Just like that. If, on the other hand, you didn't follow the directions for Kyoto after you'd been told them, you'd be certain to lose your way and wind up in an entirely different place.

So you see, you'd better listen carefully to what I say. There's no telling when I'll be back here again to talk to you, and even if you went and listened to other people, I don't think you would find anyone else who'd tell you about the unborn Buddha-mind. Be sure, then, that you don't go brewing up a lot of unnecessary thoughts in your heads. Make up your minds that you're never again going to revolve in the wheel of existence. Don't forget: If you miss the chance to become Buddhas in this life, you won't be born into the human world again, and get another chance, for millions of ages. By all means, then, you want to confirm yourselves in the unborn

Buddha-mind now and keep yourself free of illusion. When you've done that, the men will live undeluded in their men's Buddha-minds, and the women in their women's Buddha-minds—you'll all be Buddhas. Enlightened Buddhas.

And while we're on the subject of women's Buddha-minds, I know there are many women who are deeply troubled by those who say that they're cut off from Buddhahood just because they're women.[52] Nothing could be further from the truth. I'm addressing the women here now, so listen carefully. How could women be any different from men in this? Men are Buddha-beings. Women are too. You needn't doubt it for a moment. Once you've got the principle of this Unborn fixed in your minds, you're unborn whether you're a man or a woman. Men and women are not the same in appearance. We all know that. But there's not a whisker of difference between them when it comes to their Buddha-minds. So don't be deluded by outward appearances.

Here's something that will prove to you that the Buddha-mind is the same in men and women. There are a lot of people gathered here. Now, suppose that outside the temple walls someone started to beat on a drum or strike a bell. When you heard those sounds, would the women here mistake the drumbeat for the bell, or the bell for the drumbeat? No. As far as hearing those sounds is concerned, no difference exists between the men and the women. It's not only true of men and women; there are people of all kinds in this hall: old people and young, priests and laity, and so on. But there wouldn't be any difference in the way that a young person, or a monk, or a layman heard the sounds either. The place in which there's no difference in the hearing of those sounds is the Unborn, the Buddha-mind, and it's perfectly equal and absolutely the same in each one of you. When we say "This is a man" or "This is a woman," those designations result from the arising of thought. They come afterward. At the place of the Unborn, before the thought arises, attributes such as "man" or "woman" don't even exist. That should make it clear that there's no distinction between men's Buddha-minds and women's. There's no reason, then, to doubt about women having Buddha-minds.

You see, you are always unborn. You go along living in the Buddha-mind unconscious of being a man or a woman. But while you are doing that, perhaps you'll see or hear something that bothers you, perhaps someone will make a nasty remark about you, saying they don't like you, or whatever. You let your mind fasten on that, you begin to fret over it, and thoughts crowd into your mind. You may feel that you want something, or you may feel unhappy, and yet if you don't allow this to lead you astray, into thinking that it can't be helped *because you're only a woman*, then you will be able to gain a strong confirmation of the Unborn. Then you yourself are a Buddha, of the same substance not only as other men and women but also as all Buddhas of the past and future. So there are no grounds whatsoever for saying women can't become Buddhas. If they really couldn't, what would I gain by going around lying to everyone? I'd be willfully deluding you. If I was guilty of that, I'd be the first candidate for hell. I struggled very hard, from the time I was a little boy, because I wanted to become a Buddha. Now, do you think I want to fall into hell at this point for making up lies? All I've been telling you is unvarnished truth. So listen carefully, ladies. Give me your undivided attention, and you'll be able to put your minds at rest.

This subject reminds me of something that happened last year when I gave a sermon in Bizen. Among those who attended was a party of four or five people, including a couple of women, who came from Niwase [now in the city of Okayama] in the Bitchū area. One of the women sent word that she wished to ask me something. She didn't feel it was right for a woman to raise questions during the sermon itself, so she wanted to know if it would be possible to ask her questions in private.

I gladly agreed, and sometime later she arrived with three or four others. We introduced ourselves, and then the woman said: "I come from a place called Niwase. I'm married and lead a very average life. My husband and I have no children of our own, but by my husband's former wife there is a son whom I've raised. Now that he's grown, he treats me with the same consideration he would show a real mother. It's just like having a son of my own, so I'm pleased with the way things have worked out.

"But there is one thing I am concerned about. I heard that a childless woman can't become a Buddha, no matter how great her desire for the Pure Land. I've asked Buddhist priests whether it was true or not. They told me it was, that women can't attain Buddhahood. So here I am. I've had the good fortune to be born a human being, yet I'm cut off from Buddhahood. I can't help feeling that gaining human form was meaningless after all. I deplore my bad luck in being born as a woman. It's made me sick pining over it. As you can see, I've wasted away to skin and bone. I'd been longing so much to find a great priest such as yourself who could answer this question for me. I was overjoyed to hear that you would be coming here to give some talks. It was a reply to my prayers. Now, at long last, I'll be able to find out if it's true what I've always heard about childless women being incapable of attaining Buddhahood."

The people with her spoke up: "It's just as she says. The idea that childless women can't become Buddhas has been tormenting her ever since she heard about it. It worries her day and night. She hasn't really been well for several years now. She has wasted away to a shadow. There must be many childless women in the world, but surely none is more concerned about her future existence than she is. She thinks of nothing else. You can see for yourself how deeply troubled she is."

I'm glad that today's talk gave me an opportunity to tell you this story. What I said to that woman is just what I say to people everywhere I go. It's the same thing that I've been telling you, so listen carefully. To prove to her that people without children can become Buddhas, I cited the fact that in all the generations of Zen masters, beginning with the first patriarch, Bodhidharma, and continuing right up to myself, there has never been a single one of us who had children. I asked if she had ever heard that Bodhidharma or any of the others had fallen into hell. She said that although we didn't have any children, she didn't believe it possible for people like us—she said we were Buddhas—to fall into hell, no matter what we did.

"Do you mean to tell me," I said, "that the minds of childless women work differently from those of other people? You have a Buddha-mind, regardless of your sex. When you hear the sound of a bell, there's no difference in the way that Buddhas, patriarchs, me, you, or anyone else hears it. If you really want to be born as a Buddha, you can. Anyone who says you can't is wrong. It's as simple as that."

"Your words are reassuring," she said, "but it's still hard for me to forget all that talk about women being barred from Buddhahood."

"But just think of all the women who have become Buddhas since the time of Shakamuni Buddha. Haven't you heard
about King Prasenajit's daughter Srimala? Or the eight-year-
old Naga maiden? In China, there was Ling-chao, the daughter
of Layman P'ang. In Japan, there was Taima Chūjōhime.[53] All
of them became Buddhas. So who is there to say that you
can't?"

That convinced her. "You don't know how glad I am to hear
that," she said. "You've rid me of doubts that have been tormenting me for years."

She stayed on for a while in Bizen and attended my talks.
Her appetite returned to normal and her spirits picked up.
Her companions were all amazed and overjoyed to see her
back to her old self. Isn't it remarkable how such an aspiration
awakened in a woman and became the central concern in her
life? That's why I told you her story. I want you to have that
same kind of aspiration in your minds too.

Furthermore, even wicked people aren't deprived of the
Buddha-mind; all they have to do is change their minds, go
back to the Buddha-mind, and they're living in the Unborn.
Let me give you another example.

Two men are walking toward the city of Takamatsu. One is
a good man and the other an evil man, though of course neither of them is conscious of that. As they walk on engaged in
conversation on a variety of subjects, if something occurs
along the road, they will see it, though they have no thought
to do so. The things they come upon appear equally to the
eyes of the good man and the evil man. If a horse or a cow approaches from the opposite direction, both men will step
aside to let it pass. They step aside, even if they are conversing
at the time, despite the fact that neither man has made up his
mind beforehand to do so. If there is a ditch they must jump

over, they both jump over it. When they come to a stream, they both ford it.

You might suspect that the good man would step aside to let the horse or cow pass without prior reflection, whereas the evil man would not be able to do so as readily, that is, without some deliberation, but the fact is, there isn't the slightest difference between them in performing this act. It shows that the unborn Buddha-mind is found even in an evil man.

Until now, the basic inclination of your minds has been to thoughts of regret, desire, and so forth; you've been losing your tempers, getting angry, turning your Buddha-minds into the way of the fighting spirits or hungry ghosts, and moving deludedly through the wheel of existence. Despite that, if you listen to me here today and come to understand what I tell you, those same regretful, desire-filled minds will become, willy-nilly, the minds of Buddhas, and you won't miss out on your Buddha-minds ever again. In other words, you'll become living Buddhas. Be very careful, then, for if you fail to regain your Buddha-mind, if you fail to realize it in this lifetime, you won't have another chance for millions and millions of ages. So you'd better be sure that what I've been telling you is fixed well in your minds.

I think I'll be getting on to bed now. You should be going back, too.

The twenty-sixth day of the eighth month— the morning sermon

All of the people here want to become Buddhas. That's what brought you to this hall so early in the morning. It's a good thing you have come, because if you fail to become Buddhas now, you won't have another chance for thousands upon thousands of ages. You were born into the human world for one reason—so you could become Buddhas. If you miss this chance and fall into hell, much greater suffering awaits you, as you transmigrate endlessly, being born and dying over and over again, through many lives, in many different worlds. Now, no one wants that to happen to them, so you'd better be sure you understand what I say very, very well.

You may have encountered men who, in their ill-used worldly wisdom, say that people are taught that they will be born into heaven or hell after they die simply to intimidate them. Anyone who would say something so thoughtless obviously hasn't a shred of understanding about what the real Buddha Way is like. Now, if someone did come along whose teaching somehow compared with Shakamuni's, and he denied the existence of hell and paradise, we might give some weight to what he said. But from the mouth of a man whose wisdom doesn't extend beyond the tip of his glib tongue, how can such words help being woefully mistaken?

In the first place, Shakamuni possessed all six supernatural powers. He could employ skillful means at will.[54] He knew all about both hell and paradise without having to move from where he sat. He traveled to many places to preach his Dharma. It spread over India, passed into China, and from there came to Japan. We now find it recorded in a great many sutras. Along comes a man who hasn't the faintest notion about any of this to declare that the Buddhas, their teaching, the Buddhist Dharma itself, none of it exists. He's like a summer insect that never lives to see the winter and imagines that the world is always hot.

Shakamuni is a Buddha whose name has been known to all the generations that came after him—in China, India, and Japan. Would such a man have preached that hell and paradise exist if they didn't? What would have been gained by that? Now, if the worldly-wise want to believe that paradise and hell don't exist, that's their business. The least they can do is keep their ideas to themselves. It's intolerable to have them arrogantly spreading such groundless nonsense to others.

Now, I'm sure you've all seen it happen—when everyone praises a person who has some exceptional skill in an art or trade, there will always be some self-important fellow who will try to deny the general opinion and belittle that person's skill. What words can describe such petty meanness? If someone they themselves take a fancy to has some trifling talent not even worth mentioning, these same fellows will invariably praise him to the skies. There are a great many such people around. It's easy to see how wrong they are. When you praise someone, you should praise him so as to please him, and when you hear about someone else's happiness, you should be happy yourself, just as if something good had happened to you. That's the proper way for people to live in the world. It is also the condition of the Unborn. When everything is seen and heard with a selfish bias, your inherent Buddha-mind—the very Buddha-mind that your parents gave you when you were born—is turned into a hell. It's deplorable that anyone would change it into a fighting spirit or hell because of an egotistic partiality for himself. It would be the most unfilial thing you could do.

No parent wants his child to grow into a scoundrel or good-for-nothing, the object of people's hatred, to see him punished by the law, maybe even destined for the executioner's blade. Unless you make an earnest effort to set yourself straight, you shouldn't even talk of filial piety. All of you should make up your minds to begin today, for really, there's nothing so wonderful as the care and affection of a parent for his child. Your parents looked after you when you didn't know what was going on around you. They raised you until you could think for yourself. You didn't know the first thing about Buddhism. Now you've heard its wonderful teachings and come to learn about the unborn Buddha-mind. Think about it. It was possible because of deep parental love. To honor your parents for all they've done for you is the behavior natural to a good son or daughter. When you are in accord with the way of filial piety, your mind is the Buddha-mind. Don't think because we speak of a mind of filial piety and a Buddha-mind that they represent two different minds. There's only the one single mind, and it's directly conversant with all things.

Detach yourself from a self-interested way of thinking, which will make you lose your temper and make you feel unhappy over this and crave after that. And don't be hard on your servants. Treat them kindly too. Just because you pay them a wage doesn't entitle you to strike them or speak to them in an unreasonable manner. You shouldn't regard them as strangers. Think of them as members of your family.

Children often disobey their parents when their parents tell them what to do. When the disobedient child belongs to someone else, it irritates you no end. When it's your own child, however, you put up with his antics because you think of him as yours. No matter how unreasonable you are in reprimanding your own offspring, because you are his parent he probably will not resent it too deeply. But the resentment a servant will feel, because he is not related to you, is an altogether different matter.

If until now you've been losing your temper, scolding people, and upsetting yourself, without even thinking much about it, you've been deeply mistaken. You've been unaware of the reason for it, so you've gone along under the delusion that anger is one of the norms of society. But from now on, inasmuch as you've been told how to become unborn, you shouldn't do anything that will incapacitate your Buddha-mind. And by the way, don't get the idea that your servants put me up to saying this, because they didn't.

It doesn't matter how inept a servant may be, if you lose your temper, and with it your Buddha-mind, you know the result—it's just as I've been telling you. And it's no different if you are a servant. If servants attend faithfully to their duties, and don't give their master reason to be displeased with them or let him down through some discreditable act, then they will have everyone's praise, their master will be disposed kindly toward them, they'll be acting dutifully toward their parents, and it will benefit them as well. So servants, too, should keep what I say firmly in mind.

Women are unlike men in being straightforward about things. They may be more frivolous than men in their basic dispositions, yet when you tell them that they will go to hell if they do something evil, they understand it right away, without any skepticism. And when you tell them they will become Buddhas if they do good, their thoughts turn single-mindedly to becoming Buddhas—and their attainment of faith is all the deeper. When they hear my teaching of the Unborn and come to be convinced of it, women in their simple directness are the ones that become Buddhas, rather than men with their shrewd intellectuality.

But some of you may be thinking: "Bankei keeps telling us not to be angry, not to let ourselves feel happy, and so on. Always watch your step. Practice self-control. But if we were doing that, and someone began to ridicule us, calling us a fool, we wouldn't be able to stand for that and agree with him and say, 'Yes, I'm a fool.' "

Now, I can understand your reasoning, but someone who would call another person a fool when he's not is himself rather foolish. You should overlook what such a person says. Don't pay any attention to it.

A samurai, however, would not tolerate that kind of talk from anyone. Let me use an illustration. Many people own expensive pieces of pottery—Korean tea bowls, flower vases, and so on. I don't have any of them myself, but I see those others have collected. They wrap the articles up carefully in layers of the softest cloth and keep them in boxes, which is understandable, since if one of those precious pieces were to strike against something hard, it might break, and the owner certainly wouldn't want that to happen. Carefully protecting the objects in this way with silk and cotton wrappings is an effective method of keeping them from being damaged.

A samurai's disposition is like that. He always places his sense of honor and self-respect above all else. If he hears even a word that seems to run counter to this, he calls the speaker to account without an instant's hesitation. Once a word of challenge has passed between two samurai, there can be no question of them letting the matter drop, so they always make sure beforehand to keep this hard, uncompromising side of their mind carefully under wraps, so its rough, abrasive edges won't come into contact with others. Once a challenge has been spoken between two samurai, the matter isn't resolved until one of them has fallen.

Sometimes, while spearheading an attack, a samurai will cut down an adversary by rushing in front of his master to shield him from danger. When it's done by a samurai, we don't regard such an act as murder. It would be if he were to kill someone from a selfish personal motive. In that case, his

Buddha-mind is turned into a fighting spirit. Again, if they don't die for their lord when their duty calls for it, if they flee or retreat or show even a hint of what may be construed as cowardice, then their Buddha-mind is transformed into an animal. Now, birds and animals don't have human intelligence and can't tell right from wrong, so they have no conception of a sense of duty or doing what is right. They don't even think about such things. They only run from danger when it approaches and do their best to preserve their lives. So for a samurai to forget his sense of duty and run shamefully from the midst of his comrades, instead of attacking the enemy, would make him no different from an animal.

I have a temple in Edo, located in Azabu on the outskirts of the city.[55] We once had a man there who worked around the temple. He had an interest in religious matters to begin with, I think, for he was always observing the daily lives of the monks. From this, a genuine religious aspiration must have developed in him naturally. In any case, one evening some of the monks sent him on an errand that took him to the outer fringes of the city, where houses were few and far between. It was an area where from time to time a samurai wanting to try the edge of his blade on a human body had been appearing and cutting down passing travelers.[56] The monks were concerned for his safety because it was getting dark and he would have to pass through this dangerous area. But he told them not to worry, and he set right out, saying that he would be back soon. As the messenger returned in the growing darkness, however, sure enough the samurai stepped out at his usual haunt and brushed past him.

"You brushed your sleeve against me on purpose," he growled, drawing his sword.

"But my sleeve didn't even touch you," replied the messenger. Then, for some reason, he prostrated himself before the samurai three times. The samurai, who had raised his sword and was on the point of striking, now unaccountably lowered it.

"You're a strange one," he said. "Well, go on, I'll let you pass." And the messenger escaped unharmed.

Now, a tradesman had seen all this take place. He had fled to the safety of a nearby roadside teahouse and had witnessed the events from his place of hiding.

When he saw the sword about to fall, he turned his eyes away and waited fearfully for the inevitable to happen. When he finally looked up again, he saw to his surprise that the messenger was standing right before him.

"You certainly got out of that by the skin of your teeth!" he said. He then asked the messenger what had made him think to give the three bows.

The messenger answered that all the people where he worked bowed three times. "My mind was completely empty. I just thought, If you're going to strike me with that sword, then do it. I made those bows without thinking. The man told me I was a strange fellow and said he would spare me. Then he allowed me to go past."

So, having barely escaped death, the messenger returned safely to the temple. I told him that I thought this was because of the depth of his religious mind, which enabled him to reach the heart of such a lawless samurai. It goes to show that nothing is more trustworthy than the Buddhist Dharma.

I run across various things in my travels around the country. I have a temple in Ōzu, in Iyo Province, where I spend some time almost every year.[57] Unlike here, the buildings are large, and whenever I visit, great crowds assemble. There is one hall especially for women and another for men. I have two men and two women whose job is to see that the seating of the audience goes smoothly. They also make sure everyone listens as he or she should. People from the countryside two or three miles around Ōzu come to take part in the meetings.

At one of these meetings was a young woman from Ōzu who was married to a man from a place several miles outside the city. His mother was living with them, and they had one child, but the marriage wasn't going well. They were constantly bickering. Then there was a great quarrel, and the wife decided to turn her child over to her husband and return to her parents' home. As she was about to leave, her husband picked up the small infant and threatened to throw him into the river unless she changed her mind.

"He's all yours," she retorted. "I don't care what you do to him."

"Go on and leave then," her husband replied. "But I won't let you take any clothing with you or anything else!"

"You can have them," she said. "All I want is to get away from here." And she set off for her parents' house in Ōzu.

Now, at that very time, a large group of men and women were leaving for the temple to listen to one of my talks. Seeing them, the woman decided to join them; instead of going straight home to her parents, she came to the temple and listened intently to the talk I gave that day. When it was over, she fell in with the procession of people making their way home. On the road, she happened to meet one of her parents' neighbors, who asked her what she was doing in Ōzu.

"I had a quarrel with my husband this morning, and left the house," she said. "I had come this far, when I noticed these people going to hear a priest give a sermon. It seemed a good opportunity, so instead of going straight to my parents, I went with them to the temple. The sermon I heard today seemed to be directed at me personally. I'm so ashamed. It was my own ill-natured disposition that made me leave my husband's house today. He didn't want me to leave. He and my mother-in-law both tried to talk me out of it. But I was in a great temper over some trifle and wouldn't listen to them. I made them both very angry. But today's sermon made me realize how wrong I've been. I'm not going home to my parents. I'm going straight back to my husband, let him know how much I regret what I've done, and beg him and my mother-in-law for their forgiveness. And I must tell them about the wonderful sermon I heard; unless I can get them to understand about transmigration too, my own learning about it will be for nothing."

After hearing her story, the neighbor said, "It sounds as if you've had a serious quarrel. Now that matters have reached this point, I don't see how you can just go home. No, I can't let you return by yourself. Go on to your parents' house. Later, I'll go with you and help you patch things up with your husband."

"There's no need for that," she said. "Whatever happens, the fault was all mine. I'll try to soothe their anger and get back in their good graces. After that, I must tell them about the wonderful teaching I heard today. It's not for me alone. It's something to share with them. Then it will have real meaning."

Others in the group, who had been listening to this exchange as they walked along, were amazed. "What a remarkable young woman. She only heard the priest's teaching today, and already she's repenting her mistake. You certainly don't see that happen often, especially in a woman!"

They scolded the neighbor: "Why are you trying to stop her

when she says she wants to go home alone? Telling her you'll help her patch things up! You should be ashamed. You live here in Ōzu, you must have heard the priest's teaching many times. How could you give her such bad advice?

"You have the right idea," they told the woman. "You should hurry right back to your husband." So she set off immediately for her home.

That same day, I was invited to someone's house in Ōzu. A number of his friends were also there. They told me the woman's story and marveled that today's sermon had worked to such great effect. Afterward, I learned the rest of the story. It seems that, on arriving home, this is what the wife said to her husband and mother-in-law:

"You didn't tell me to leave. My stupidity and foul disposition were the cause of it all. They made me oppose you, they made me obstinately insist on leaving to go back to my parents. But as it turned out, my leaving must have been arranged by the Buddhas themselves to set me on the right path. I met some people who were on their way to hear a priest give a sermon. I joined them and went to the temple. Everything the priest said applied directly to me. It was as if every word was spoken to me personally. It made me realize how wrong my thoughts had been. So after I left the meeting, I decided to come right back here to you. It was my mean disposition and nothing else that was responsible for causing the two of you this distress. In the future, I'll do just as you tell me. Please, take out all your anger on me. Do whatever you want, it doesn't matter. I've said what I wanted to say. However hard my lot becomes, I won't feel the least resentment ever again."

When they heard this, the husband and mother-in-law were more than glad to have her back. "It was an unimportant matter that caused you to lose your temper. You know now that it was wrong. You've come back. There's nothing more to say about it."

So things worked out much better than before. She became an obedient wife and a respectful daughter-in-law and devoted herself diligently to her kitchen work. From time to time, she told them about the wonderful teaching of the Unborn, and before long she had persuaded them to come and hear me. During my visits to that area, the three of them attended regularly.

Isn't it commendable that a person who has ties to Buddha like this woman—an ordinary woman with no intellectual pretensions—can come to have a mind free of all contentiousness and anger, just by listening to me once? I wanted all of you to hear this story. I hope it will serve as an example to you and will prompt you to get on the right path and live in the Unborn too.

I've probably tired you out with this long talk today. Let's stop here. I hope to see you again at tomorrow's meeting.

The first day of the ninth month—
the morning sermon

I'm very pleased that you've all gathered here before daylight to hear what I have to say, despite being squeezed together into this crowded hall. Each of you left your bed while it was still dark outside to come here because you wanted to become a Buddha. What prompted you to come was the natural wisdom that you are born with. In other words, you came because of the working of your Buddha-mind. Although you each have a Buddha-mind, you've deprived yourselves of it because of the mistaken way that you've been brought up. A lifetime of learning the wrong things. You still have a Buddha-mind, for all the bad things you've learned and the delusions your thoughts create for you. You can't possibly lose it. It's just darkened by the illusions caused by your selfish desires and partiality.

Perhaps a comparison will help make this clear. The sun shines day after day without fail, yet if clouds appear to make the sky overcast, it can't be seen. It still comes up in the east every morning and goes down in the west. The only difference is that you can't see it because it's hidden behind the clouds. The sun is your Buddha-mind, the clouds are your illusions. You are unaware of your Buddha-mind because it's covered by illusions and can't be seen. But you never lose it, not even when you go to sleep. The unborn Buddha-mind that your mother gave you is thus always there, wonderfully clear and bright and illuminating. Right at the moment that you're born into the world, if someone were to throw cold water over you, you'd feel cold. If you put your fingers near a fire, you'd feel hot—that's all due to the working of this same Buddha-mind. It takes care of everything. It makes everything go smoothly.

Pride and self-assertiveness are traits found in many people. They can't bear to be second to anyone. It's wrong to be that way, of course, but that's what pride does to you. If you aren't always thinking about getting the best of others, then you'll never have to worry about being second to them either. If people treat you badly, the reason is your own self-seeking ways. If they are disagreeable to you, it's because there is something disagreeable about you yourself. If you turn your thoughts from those others and direct them to yourself, you'll find that there isn't a single bad person anywhere on earth.

When anger arises in your mind, you change the marvelous wisdom of your Buddha-mind into the way of the hungry ghosts or fighting spirits. Anger and happiness both exist only because of your partiality to yourself. This partiality makes you lose the Buddha-mind's marvelous wisdom and sends you into the endless illusion of the wheel of existence. If it disappears, however, your mind becomes the mind of the Unborn, and you do not transmigrate. That's why it's so important for you to understand about your Buddha-mind. Once you have, then, even without performing a lot of religious disciplines, you're unborn that very day. If the Buddha-mind is clearly realized, that's enough. You need do nothing else—no practice, no precepts, no zazen or koan study. Nothing like that. You'll be free from care, everything will be taken care of, just by being as you are.

If we compare the duties of a Buddhist priest with those of a samurai, we find that in some respects the duties of a samurai are easier to perform. Those who leave home to become priests usually begin their studies at an early age. Their practice takes them all over the country, even overseas to other lands. Though they may have some destination in mind, they never know what will be waiting for them when they arrive. They carry no food or money with them on their pilgrimages, and wherever they go, they find very little in the way of comfort. If someone offers them shelter while they're on the road, they accept it gratefully, regarding it as a dispensation bestowed on them by the Buddhas. When there is no such shelter, they lie down in the fields or in the mountains. If they run out of food, they take their bowl and beg for some. Often no alms are given, so they must go with an empty stomach. As a rule, their practice is carried on in a state of perpetual hunger. Occasionally, someone may give them nice lodgings. They are deeply grateful and filled with a feeling of indebtedness for this expression of the Buddhas' favor.

After the hardships they experience during this period of

pilgrimage, they may have the good fortune to receive a hermitage of their own. Or they may be entrusted with an entire temple and receive the contributions their parishioners provide. This puts them in a position of some security. But they didn't leave their homes and family and join the priesthood because they desired to achieve such comforts. All their hard, painful practice was for only one reason: They hoped to find some way to awaken themselves in enlightenment and discover the Buddha-mind.

Now, compare this life with the life of a samurai. He receives a stipend from his lord. He carries out his duties wearing warm clothing, eating regular meals, and living his daily life much as he pleases. If, as is to be hoped, he devotes some of his time to the matter of his future existence, it doesn't involve a great deal of trouble for him. Moreover, if he attains the mind of the Unborn, that will be consistent with his loyalty to his lord. Since the working of the Buddha-mind is something that extends to all things, including the samurai's duties, he won't find the routine of his work tiresome or difficult in any way. No matter what duty he may be given to perform, he does it easily in the Unborn, without any trouble. Since if he dwells in the Unborn, he isn't hindered by any thoughts of self-interest, his mind is always fair and impartial. This will be greatly appreciated by all those he comes into contact with. Any official of the shogunate who is able to bring such satisfaction to the people he deals with cannot help being a good servant to his lord. Everyone is bound to sing his praises. If in all his duties he dwells in the Unborn and takes his outlook from the Buddha Dharma, then even as a samurai his practice of the Way will be extremely beneficial to him. And it will be easier for him to practice it than for a Buddhist priest.

Or consider the difficult life of a peddler who travels

around the country carrying his wares upon his shoulders.[58] He takes his pack up and begins his day in the early hours of the morning, traveling through fields and over hills and valleys. Such a life is not easy, but set beside the practice of someone disciplining himself to become a priest, the adversity he faces is of an entirely different order. The peddler has a dwelling from which he departs on his daily rounds. It's true that he has to set out before dawn, when the stars are still out. In the evening, his clothing is soaked through with dew. But when he has sold all his wares, he can rest his weary body leisurely at an inn. His time is his own. He can forget about his daily routine and enjoy life to the extent his circumstances permit.

A priest has no real home. He can't settle anywhere. He sleeps in the open fields or in the hills. For him, there's only hardship and hunger. No one is waiting for him where he goes. There's never a moment of relief from his hard life. With only his ordinary robes and no extra clothing, he has no way to keep himself warm in cold weather. No, I don't think anything can begin to compare with the privations a priest experiences.

Still, he carries on his practice, taxing his body severely, and for one reason: because he wants to discover the wonderful bliss of the Buddha-mind. When his practice is completed, he teaches others, and he receives from them donations and benefits of various kinds. His years of painful practice are then all transformed into the Dharma, and he lives in the wonderful knowledge of the unborn Buddha-mind.

I'm going to tell you a story now that will give you an idea of the Buddha-mind's marvelous working. About thirty years ago, there was a tradesman—he later became my disciple—

whom people called Magoemon the Thief, because he used to rake in a healthy profit by overcharging in his sales. Wherever he went, people would point their fingers at him and say, "There goes that thief Magoemon." Since he had a knack for this kind of profit making, he got better and better at it, until he became a very wealthy man. Even at that time, he frequented my temple, and I used to remonstrate with him. "You're incorrigible, Magoemon. Everyone comes around here saying that you're a thief. And it's your own fault. You've only yourself to blame."

Magoemon didn't agree. "I'd feel ashamed if I'd broken into someone's home to steal their property or opened a hole in their storehouses to take something from them. But I don't rob people like that. Remember, I'm not the only one who makes a profit through trade. The people who say bad things about me, you'll notice, are most of them tradesmen themselves. They don't make the kind of money I do, so they slander me and try to cause me trouble. But the way I see it, business is business." And he remained unconcerned about it all.

Then later, I don't know what happened to cause the change in him, but he turned his business over to his nephews, took all the money he had hoarded, divided it among his kinfolk, and came to me begging me to shave his head and make him a monk.

"If anyone else had come making that request," I told him, "I might hesitate before granting it. But from someone like you, with your bad reputation, it must have been spoken with a special resolve." So I proceeded at once to turn him into a monk. He developed into a man of strong faith. This story shows the marvelous way that the Buddha-mind works. As for Magoemon, after he became a monk, not thirty days had passed before people were calling him "Buddha Magoemon." That's the way these things happen. I want each one of you here to grasp this and arrive at a firm understanding in your own minds—because one thing you may be very sure of: There's nothing in the world as wonderful as your Buddha-mind.

The only way any of you can become unborn and realize the Buddha-mind is to confirm what I'm telling you in your own mind. I won't tell you that you have to practice such and such, that you have to uphold certain rules or precepts or read certain sutras or other Zen writings, or that you have to do zazen. I'm not going to try to give you the Buddha-mind either—you already have it. If you listen carefully to me, and grasp the Buddha-mind that's already yours, then you become a genuine living Buddha. Wherever you are standing, that place is the Unborn. Whatever you want to do, you can do it. If you want to recite sutras or do zazen, observe precepts, recite the Nembutsu or the Daimoku, you should do it.[59] If you're a farmer or a tradesman and you want to work your farm or your business, then go ahead, do it; whatever it is, that will be your personal samadhi. My part in this is simply to tell you about it and to try to get you to confirm the Buddha-minds you were all given when you were born.

When daimyo from different parts of the country invite me to give talks in their areas, I always go. I'll go anywhere that I'm asked. Sometimes, the meetings last for twenty or thirty days. But wherever I go, I find that a great many people come to listen. Later, when I return, they always tell me that the number of people interested in religion seems to have grown and that there has been a noticeable improvement in public morality as well. I want you to know how glad I am that you in this area have been coming here early every morning to attend these meetings and listening so attentively to what I say. The day after tomorrow, on the third of the month, I must leave Marugame, so tomorrow morning's talk will be the last.

NOTES TO THE DHARMA TALKS

1. Butchi Kōsai is the honorary title given Bankei by imperial edict in 1690. The long winter retreat lasted from the fifth day of the tenth month of the third year of Genroku (1690) to the fifth day of the first month of the next year. These are transcriptions of some of the sixty talks and sermons he gave during the retreat.

2. These represent all the main schools of Mahayana Buddhism in Japan.

3. The three terms "Buddha-mind," "the Unborn," and "illuminative wisdom" recur throughout the talks. The "Buddha-mind" (*Busshin* in Japanese) is a synonym for the Buddha-nature that is inherent in every person, the mind as it really is, in its original state of true reality or suchness (*tathatā*), which is prior to human intellection and discrimination. In Buddhism in general, "unborn" (*fushō* in Japanese), or as it usually occurs in a pair, "unborn, undying," stands in contrast to birth and death, or samsara, the continuous process of generation and extinction to which a human is bound because of his illusion. In this sense, the Unborn may be said to be synonymous with nirvana and untouched by the vicissitudes of birth and death. "[Marvelously bright] illuminative wisdom" (*reimei* in Japanese) attempts to express in English the marvelous brightness, purity, and clarity of the Buddha-mind working in the unborn state, which Bankei elsewhere calls the "discrimination of non-discrimination" and which is totally beyond all logical calculation. This working is likened to a bright, resplendent mirror that reflects whatever comes before it exactly as it is in its reality. As no one English translation

can convey adequately these meanings contained in the word *reimei*, I have found it necessary to render it in various ways. For Suzuki's brief discussion of the term, see *Kenkyū*, pp. 21–23.

4. An appellation given to a Buddha when he appears in this world; literally, it means "one who is thus come"; a living Buddha.

5. An incalculable length of time, an age.

6. The Buddha-mind sect (*Busshin-shū* in Japanese) as a name for the Zen school first appears in the records of Bodhidharma, the first Zen patriarch in China, *Dentō-roku, ch.* 2.

7. The words "unborn, undying" appear, for example, in the *Heart Sutra* and in the celebrated Buddhist philosopher Nagarjuna's (second or third century) eightfold negation: nonbirth, nonextinction, noncessation, nonpermanence, nonuniformity, nondiversity, noncoming, nongoing.

8. Three time periods were supposed to follow the Buddha's death: the period of the *right Dharma*, when the Buddhist teaching, practice, and enlightenment exist; the period of the *semblance* or *imitative Dharma*, when teaching and practice alone remain; and the *latter* or *final Dharma*, when only the teaching remains and people are unable either to practice it or to gain enlightenment. In Japan, "latter-day" teachings began to appear at the end of the Heian period (794–1185), when, according to one theory, the age of the semblance Dharma ended and the final age began. By Bankei's lifetime, the world was generally assumed to be well into the final period.

9. Turning students to the Unborn by merely "commenting on their personal concerns" (in Japanese, *mi no ue no hihan*) is a characteristic feature of Bankei's Zen teaching.

10. In the Buddhist conception, living beings are classified into ten worlds or realms: those of the hell-dwellers, hungry or craving ghosts, animals, fighting spirits, humans, heavenly beings, hearers of the Buddha's teaching, private Buddhas, bodhisattvas, and Buddhas. The first six of these are the lesser ways; beings in these various states of illusion

are subject to transmigration in the wheel of existence. The last four are the enlightened realms of the saintly beings. The first three of the six lesser ways, called the three evil ways, are regarded as especially unfavorable rebirth destinations. The hell-dwellers constantly undergo a variety of torments in the different realms of hell; the craving ghosts suffer from constant, unappeasable hunger and thirst; the animals are characterized by ignorance; the fighting spirits, or *ashura*, live in perpetual strife; heavenly beings live in constant happiness and know no suffering but are thus never conduced to any awakening of religious aspiration. With both suffering and pleasure in degree, the human realm alone among the six ways contains the possibility of religious aspiration and attainment of Buddhahood.

11. Dōsha Chōgen (Chinese Tao-che Ch'ao-yuan; 1600?–1661?); see Notes to the Introduction, number 17.

12. The Japanese term is *jittoku*, for a short, hip-length robe worn over the regular kimono in the Edo period (1603–1867); used by such people as Confucian scholars, retired monks, and lay Buddhists.

13. *Great Learning* (*Ta-hsueh* in Chinese; *Daigaku* in Japanese), one of the four classic books of Confucianism. This famous passage appears at the very beginning. See Introduction, p. 5.

14. Bankei refers to his teacher Umpo Zenjō.

15. The constant repetition of the formula "Namu-Amida-Butsu" ("Homage to Amida Buddha"; also called Nembutsu) leading to samadhic concentration and unity with Amidha Buddha is a practice espoused by the Pure Land schools and the Jōdo sect in particular. As a boy, Bankei spent time at a temple of the Pure Land Shin sect. See Introduction, p. 6.

16. *Omoyu* in Japanese, this broth, consisting of the liquid drawn off from rice gruel, is traditional food for invalids and sick people who can take no other sustenance.

17. Gudō Tōshoku (1579–1661) was one of the leading Rinzai Zen figures of his day. Itsuzan, in the *Ryakki*, calls Gudō "the foremost master in the land." *Goroku*, p. 226.

18. In the biographies, the identity of these priests is given variously as Sekiō, Ryōdō, and Mitsuun; the last was a disciple of Gudō Tōshoku's. See Notes to the Introduction, number 15.

19. Lying is one of the five cardinal evils of Buddhism, along with taking life, stealing, adultery, and drinking intoxicants.

20. "Heresy" refers to any non-Buddhist teaching. Christianity was introduced into Japan by Francis Xavier and other priests from the middle of the sixteenth century: The years 1549–1650 have been called the "Christian century" of Japan. Beginning in the early seventeenth century, Japanese government policy changed. A period of suppression of Christianity and persecution of its adherents began, which ended in a complete proscription. George Sansom, in his *History of Japan, 1615–1867*, p. 102, cites a document, dated 1658, containing various governmental prohibitions; one states: "In rural districts not a single Christian priest or brother or other member of a forbidden sect may be allowed entry. Care must be taken to prevent such entry."

21. The beginning of the twelfth month is traditionally the start of the Rōhatsu *sesshin* in Zen temples, a period of intensive practice; it ends on the morning of the eighth day, the time when Shakamuni is traditionally thought to have attained his enlightenment.

22. Greed, anger, and foolishness or ignorance are called "poisons" because they are the source of all human passions and illusions.

23. See note 7.

24. Ingen (1592–1673) was a Chinese priest (his name in Chinese is Yin-yuan Lung-ch'i) and founder of the Ōbaku Zen school in Japan. Bankei is not known to have been in Nagasaki in the summer of 1654, when Ingen arrived. Apparently, either there is a mistake in the transcription here, or else Bankei himself confused Ingen for Ingen's disciple Mokuan, who arrived in Nagasaki in 1655, when Bankei was there visiting Dōsha. See Introduction, p. 18 and Notes to the Introduction, number 26.

25. A central Mahayana Buddhist concept: Deluded samsaric existence is, as such, nirvana, the perfectly tranquil state of enlightenment.

26. One stick of incense lasts approximately thirty minutes. *Kinhin*, sometimes called walking zazen, means walking about during periods of meditation to relieve fatigue or drowsiness.

27. "Old tools" refers primarily to koans.

28. The great ball (or lump, or mass) of doubt (in Japanese, *daigidan*) is "the state of mind reached by the koan student when he has pursued the koan up to a certain stage. . . . It is a kind of mental blockade . . . [in which] the stream of thought is blocked up . . . does not run on but is frozen and forms a lump." Daisetz Suzuki, *Living by Zen,* p. 221.

29. Bankei refers here to the distinction made between the teaching of the Pure Land school, which holds that enlightenment is attained solely through the compassionate power of an "other," Amida Buddha, and other schools, such as Zen, which hold that it is achieved through the self-effort of each practicer.

30. There is a well-known exchange similar to this one between Hui-k'o and Bodhidharma. See Zenkei Shibayama, *Zen Comments on the Mumonkan,* case 41.

31. Bankei alludes to the well-known maxim attributed to Bodhidharma that describes the principles of the Zen sect: "Kyōge betsuden, furyū monji, jikishi ninshin, kenshō jōbutsu." This states that Zen is "a special transmission outside the Buddhist scriptures, not based on words or letters, in which one sees into one's true nature and attains Buddhahood by directly pointing to one's own [Buddha-] mind."

32. The three evil realms (in Japanese, *san-akudō*) are the three lowest and least desirable rebirths in the wheel of existence: the realms of hell, hungry ghosts, and animals. See note 10.

33. "Indifferent" translates the Buddhist technical term *muki* (Sanskrit *avyākrta*). *Muki* is used in conjunction with *zenki* ("good") and *akuki* ("bad") to refer to what is neutral, indifferent, or neither good nor bad. The English word "indifferent," although admittedly inadequate, does, I think, convey the basic sense of *muki* as it is being used here. The monk imagines that dwelling in what Bankei calls the unborn Buddha-mind would mean entering into a zombielike state of indeter-

minate, anesthetic inactivity, cut off from feeling and sensation. See *Living by Zen,* p. 224.

34. The thief earned his sobriquet from being so elusive; the *kappa* is a type of Japanese water imp.

35. Kumasaka Chōhan, a famous robber who figures in the stories of the twelfth-century wars between the Taira and Genji clans. According to one legend, he went to the great monastery at Mount Kōya intending to steal but instead realized his evil ways and became a priest of deep faith.

36. During the Edo period (1603–1867), criminals were often recruited from among the inmates in the prisons to work as agents (*meakashi*).

37. According to the Pure Land schools of Japanese Buddhism, the calling of the formula "Namu-Amida-Butsu" (or Nembutsu) brings salvation and rebirth in the Pure Land of Bliss through the grace of Amida Buddha.

38. One of the six "supernatural" powers attained by Buddhas is the ability to see into others' minds (*tashinzū* in Japanese). See note 54.

39. "Hyakujō's Fox" is a famous koan, found in the popular koan collection *Mumonkan* (in Chinese, *Wu-men kuan*), case 2. See Shibayama, pp. 33–44.

40. The priest alludes to the "Triple Invalid" koan, which appears in the *Hekiganroku*, case 88. In it, the T'ang priest Gensha Shibi (Chinese, Hsuan-sha Shih-pei) speaks these words to his disciples:

All masters speak about their office of ministering for the sake of living beings. How would you deal with a triple invalid if he should appear suddenly before you here? You may hold up a mallet or a fly whisk, but a man suffering from blindness cannot see you. You could give play to all the verbal resources at your command, but a man suffering from deafness cannot hear you. You may let him tell you his understanding, but that is impossible since he is mute. How, then, will you deal with him? If you cannot deal with him, the Buddha Dharma must be pronounced wanting in spiritual efficacy.

41. The Precepts, or Vinaya (*Ritsu* in Japanese), sect bases its teaching on the strict observance of certain rules (250 rules for a priest; 500 for a nun), which is thought to lead one to enlightenment. The Precepts sect was one of the old Buddhist schools brought from China in the Nara period (646–794). Its influence greatly waned with the appearance of new schools in the Kamakura period (1192–1333).

42. Bankei refers to the term *zenchishiki*, literally a "good man," a name given to a person who helps another to make progress toward enlightenment.

43. Bankei was, like many of the great Zen teachers, a painter and calligrapher (specimens of his work fetch high prices whenever they appear). He was also an accomplished sculptor of Buddhist images; many of his works are still enshrined in the temples with which he was associated. See Fujimoto, pp. 614–15.

44. The three "worlds" (*sanze* in Japanese) refer to the past, present, and future. Attainment of Buddhahood is said to bring with it the ability to see all time and space as if you are looking at the palm of your hand.

45. Bankei had to cross the Inland Sea from the Ryūmon-ji, his main temple, to reach Marugame, a castle town on the Inland Sea coast of the island of Shikoku. Sanuki Province is present Kagawa prefecture. The Hōshin-ji was built by the lord of Marugame Castle, Kyōgoku Takatoyo, for his mother, a devoted follower of Bankei. She had passed away the previous year, and her dying wish was that Bankei lead a retreat at the Hōshin-ji. Bankei's sermons took place from the twenty-third day of the eighth month to the second day of the ninth month. He returned on the third of the month to the Ryūmon-ji to begin the long winter retreat, which opened on the fifth. Chronologically, then, the Hōshin-ji sermons were delivered before those at the Ryūmon-ji. All the main manuscript copies have the Ryūmon-ji sermons first.

46. Bankei refers to the four constituent elements of the universe. A Japanese poem attributed to Bankei reads: "This Mind is unborn and undying, Earth, water, fire, and air are its temporary home." *Goroku*, p. 181.

47. The Sanskrit word *nirvana* appears in transliterated form as the Chinese *nie-pan* or *nie-p'an*, which in Japanese becomes *ne-han*. The word is used popularly to mean "death," but that is wrong, for nirvana is regarded as putting an end to all coming into life and dying. Here Bankei's explanation of *nehan* (nirvana) as "unborn" and "undying" follows a popular etymology that was apparently current in China and Japan. Cf. *The Influence of Buddhism on the Chinese Language*, Mission Press, Newchwang, 1889.

48. The Jizō-ji, rebuilt by Bankei in 1664 on the site of an old Kamakura-period temple, was a favorite resting place to which Bankei often repaired when his chronic illness made periods of convalescence necessary. At times, he also used it for retreats. Yamashina lies just to the east of Kyoto, beyond the Awataguchi pass, the old eastern entranceway to Kyoto on the Tōkaidō road.

49. In 1692, Engelbert Kaempfer described the execution grounds in Edo: "Just before we came to Sinagawa, the place of publick executions offer'd to our view a very shocking and unpleasing sight, human heads and bodies, some tending to putrefaction, some half devour'd, lying among other dead carcasses, with multitudes of dogs, ravens, crows, and other ravenous beasts and birds, waiting to satisfy their devouring appetites upon these miserable remains." Kaempfer, vol. 3, p. 70. The condemned were spread-eagled on a cross or wooden plank and dispatched with lances. When the method of execution was beheading, the head was displayed on a pike at the execution ground before the prison gates.

50. It was customary on the anniversary of the death of a member of one's family for Buddhists to observe the occasion by eating vegetarian fare and practicing the Buddhist virtues. A day of "general abstinence"

presumably refers to the death anniversary of the shogun or some member of his family, which the entire country was expected to observe.

51. A formula recited when a person enters the Buddhist life reads: "Human form is hard to get, now I have it; the Buddha Dharma is hard to hear, now I have heard it; if I do not gain salvation in this life, when will I have this chance again? All the great multitude of beings must with wholeness of heart take their refuge in the Three Treasures: Buddha, Dharma (Law), and Sangha (Community)."

52. This idea derives originally from Indian Buddhism. In India, where the social position of women was low, the idea developed that women were unable to attain salvation as women; they had first to assume the body of a man. Although later the Mahayana teaching that all beings possess the Buddha-nature allowed to women the possibility of attaining Buddhahood, the earlier notion did not completely die out, and it is seen in the Buddhist canon, whence the idea no doubt found its way into Japan. The idea of *childless* women being cut off from Buddhahood does not have any basis in orthodox Buddhist teaching and probably represents the strong influence of Confucian ancestor worship prevalent in Tokugawa Japan.

53. Srimala, the daughter of King Prasenajit of Kosala, is the protagonist of the *Srimala Sutra*. The Naga maiden appears in the *Lotus Sutra* (Devadatta chapter), as the eight-year-old daughter of the Dragon King Sagara. After presenting the Buddha with a precious gem, she turns into a man and immediately attains Buddhahood. Ling-chao (Reishō in Japanese), the celebrated daughter of the T'ang layman Hōun (P'ang-yun in Chinese; 714–808), appears with her father in a number of episodes recorded in the Zen histories. Taima Chūjōhime is a semi-legendary eighth-century daughter of Fujiwara Toyonari. She is said to have become a nun and devoted herself to the practice of Nembutsu and, with the aid of Amida Buddha, to have embroidered a picture (known as the Taima Mandala) depicting the splendors of the Pure Land of Bliss.

54. The text is literally, "Shakamuni's six sense organs [vision, hearing, smell, taste, touch, and faculty of mind] possess the six supernatural powers." These are the six superhuman faculties acquired by a Buddha, giving him extraordinary powers of seeing, hearing, discernment, and so on, incomprehensible to unenlightened beings. His vision is such that he can see everything, from the highest heavens to the lowest hells. "Skillful means" (*upāya*) refers to the various devices a Buddhist teacher uses in instructing the unenlightened and leading them to deliverance.

55. Bankei refers to the Kōrin-ji, built for him in 1678 by the lord of Marugame Castle, Kyōgoku Takatoyo, at the behest of his mother, the nun Yōshō-ni (see note 45). The Kōrin-ji was one of Bankei's three main temples.

56. Called *tsujigiri* in Japanese, these samurai would test the edges of their swords by striking down chance wayfarers on lonely byways. A rumor current earlier in the century was that Shogun Iemitsu (1603–1651) himself indulged (incognito) in nocturnal excursions of this kind. Boxer, *The Christian Century in Japan, 1549–1650*, p. 364.

57. Ōzu was an ancient castle town in Iyo Province (present Ehime prefecture) on Shikoku. The Nyohō-ji was built for him there in 1669.

58. In 1692, just two years after Bankei spoke these words, a contemporary witness, the German physician Engelbert Kaempfer, gave this description of "hawkers and pedlers":

The crowd and throng upon the roads in this country is not a little encreas'd by numberless small retail-merchants and children of country people, who run about from morning to night, following travellers, and offering them to sale their poor, for the most part eatable merchandize; such as for instance several cakes and sweet-meats, wherein the quantity of sugar is so inconsiderable, that it is scarce perceptible, other cakes of different sorts made of flowers . . . all sorts of roots boil'd in water and salt, road-books, straw-shoes for horses and men, ropes, strings, tooth-pickers, and a multitude of other trifles made of wood, straw, reed, and bambous, such as the situation of every place affords. Kaempfer, p. 345.

59. In the Lotus (Hoke in Japanese), or Nichiren, sect, the title, or *Daimoku*, of the *Lotus Sutra*, pronounced *Myōhōrenge-kyō*, is recited by the devotee in the belief that he will thereby receive all the merits contained in the sutra.

The Dialogues of
Zen Master Bankei

The following short talks and dialogues are taken from a work entitled Butchi kōsai zenji hōgo *(The Dharma words of Zen master Butchi Kōsai, that is, Bankei), a compilation by Itsuzan Sonin (1655–1734), who served as Bankei's attendant from 1689 until his death in 1693. Itsuzan's work covers a somewhat wider time period than the preceding sermons and consists mainly of Bankei's responses to questions from his own Zen disciples and followers and from representatives of other Buddhist sects. The colophon of the manuscript copy of this work, which is preserved in the Ryūmon-ji, is dated 1730, when Itsuzan was seventy-five years old. I have used the text given in Fujimoto Tsuchishige's* Bankei zenji hōgo shū. *I have added (pp. 154–59) a number of anecdotes from other sources as well, for their intrinsic interest and for the further light they shed on Bankei's religious personality.*　　　　　　　　　　　　　　*(NW)*

A LAYMAN: I'VE HEARD YOU SAY THAT BE-cause we have foolish thoughts, we become animals, and pass from darkness to darkness cut off from Buddhahood. Yet when there's no sadness in the animal's mind, it's able to do as it likes, without any awareness of its suffering. Shouldn't that be a carefree existence after all?

Bankei: But isn't it sad to live completely unaware that

you're turning the one and only Buddha-mind that you got from your parents into the sufferings of hell? If someone beats the dog that stole a chicken the day before, the dog doesn't know it's being beaten for what it did yesterday. Just the same it howls piteously when the stick falls. As an animal, not knowing the principle of cause and effect, it undergoes an endless round of suffering. For you as a human being, whose intelligence is beyond dispute, it's a relatively easy matter to encounter a good teacher and become a Buddha. So you ought to be deeply thankful that you've had the good fortune to be born into a human body. Right at hand, then, you have a matter of incalculable importance. Don't let your time pass in vain!

A layman: Every time I clear a thought from my mind, another appears right away. Thoughts keep appearing like that without end. What can I do about them?

Bankei: Clearing thoughts from the mind as they arise is like washing away blood in blood. You may succeed in washing away the original blood, but you're still polluted by the blood you washed in. No matter how long you keep washing, the bloodstains never disappear. Since you don't know that your mind is originally unborn and undying and free of illusion, you think that your thoughts really exist, so you transmigrate in the wheel of existence. You have to realize that your thoughts are ephemeral and unreal and, without either clutching at them or rejecting them, just let them come and go of themselves. They're like images reflected in a mirror. A mirror is clear and bright and reflects whatever is placed before it. But the image doesn't remain in the mirror. The Buddha-mind is ten thousand times brighter than any mirror and is marvelously illuminative besides. All thoughts vanish tracelessly into its light.

A farmer: Since I was born with a short temper, angry thoughts come into my mind very easily. This distracts me from my work. I find it extremely difficult to remain in the Unborn. What can I do so that my mind will be in harmony with the unborn mind?

Bankei: Since the unborn Buddha-mind is something you and everyone else are born with, there's no way you can go about attaining it now for the first time. Just attend to your farmwork and have no other thoughts. That's the working of the unborn mind. You can swing your hoe while you're angry, too, for that matter. But in that case, since anger is an evil that links you to hell, your work becomes hard and onerous. When you hoe with a mind unclouded by anger and other such things, the work is easy and pleasant. It's the practice of the Buddha-mind itself, so it's unborn and undying.

A monk: It took much hard practice for the great Zen masters of the past to penetrate great enlightenment so deeply. From what I have heard, your own realization also came only after many hardships. Someone like me, who hasn't engaged in any practice or arrived at any enlightenment, couldn't possibly achieve true peace of mind simply by perceiving the necessity of living in the unborn Buddha-mind and staying just as I am.

Bankei: It's like this. A group of travelers, climbing through a stretch of high mountains, gets thirsty, and one of them strikes out and makes his way far down into the valley to fetch water. It's not easy, but he finally finds some and brings it back and gives his companions a drink. Don't those who drink without having exerted themselves quench their thirst the same as the one who did? Now, if a person refused to drink the water because he felt that doing so was wrong, there wouldn't be any way to quench his thirst.

135

My own struggle was undertaken mistakenly, because I didn't meet up with a clear-eyed master. Eventually, though, I discovered the Buddha-mind for myself; ever since, I have been telling others about theirs, so they'll know about it without going through that ordeal, just as those people drink water and quench their thirst without having to go and find it for themselves. So you see, everyone *can* use the innate Buddha-mind just as it is and achieve a trouble-free peace of mind, without resorting to any misguided austerities. Don't you think that is an invaluable teaching?

A layman: I don't question that there are no illusory thoughts in the primary mind, but just the same, there's no letup to the thoughts that come into my mind. I find it impossible to stay in the Unborn.

Bankei: Although you arrived in the world with nothing but the unborn Buddha-mind, you fell into your present deluded ways as you were growing up, by watching and listening to other people in their delusion. You picked all this up gradually, over a long period of time, habituating your mind to it, until now your deluded mind has taken over completely and works its delusion unchecked. But none of your deluded thoughts was inborn. They weren't there from the start. They cease to exist in a mind that's affirming the Unborn.

It's like a sake lover who has contracted an illness that forces him to give up drinking. He still thinks about it. Thoughts about having a few drinks still enter his mind whenever he has a chance to get his hands on some sake. But since he abstains from drinking it, his illness isn't affected and he doesn't get drunk. He stays away from it despite the thoughts that arise in his mind, and eventually he becomes a healthy man, cured of his illness. Illusory thoughts are no different. If you just let them come and let them go away, and don't put them to work or try to avoid them, then one day you'll find that they've vanished completely into the unborn mind.

A monk: I have great difficulty subduing all the desires and deluded thoughts in my mind. What should I do?

Bankei: The idea to subdue deluded thoughts is a deluded thought itself. None of those thoughts exists from the start. You conjure them up out of your own discriminations.

A visiting monk: I appreciate very much what you told us last night about everyone being born with a Buddha-mind. Still, to me it would seem that if we are this Buddha-mind, illusory thoughts shouldn't arise.

Bankei: The instant you said that, what illusion was there?

A layman: I can agree with what you say about seeing and hearing by means of the Unborn. But while we're asleep, someone may be right next to us and we don't even know it. Isn't the Unborn's influence lost then?

Bankei: What loss is there? There's nothing lost. You're just sleeping.

Bankei to his assembly: Your unborn mind is the Buddha-mind itself, and it is unconcerned with either birth or death. As evidence of this, when you look at things, you're able to see and distinguish them all at once. And as you are doing that, if a bird sings or a bell tolls, or other noises or sounds occur, you hear and recognize each of them too, even though you haven't given rise to a single thought to do so. Everything in your life, from morning until night, proceeds in this same way, without your having to depend upon thought or reflection. But most people are unaware of that; they think everything is a result of their deliberation and discrimination. That's a great mistake.

The mind of the Buddhas and the minds of ordinary men are not two different minds. Those who strive earnestly in their practice because they want to attain satori, or to discover their self-mind, are likewise greatly mistaken. Everyone who recites the *Heart Sutra* knows that "the mind is unborn and undying."[1] But they haven't sounded the *source* of the Unborn. They still have the idea that they can find their way to the unborn mind and attain Buddhahood by using reason and discrimination. As soon as the notion to seek Buddhahood or to attain the Way enters your mind, you've gone astray from the Unborn—gone against what is unborn in you. Anyone who tries to become enlightened thereby falls out of the Buddha-mind and into secondary matters. You are Buddhas to begin with. There's no way for you to become Buddhas now for the first time. Within this original mind, there isn't even a trace of illusion. Nothing, I can assure you, ever arises from within it. When you clench your fists and run about, for example—that's the Unborn. If you harbor the least notion to become better than you are or the slightest inclination to seek something, you turn your back on the Unborn. There's neither joy nor anger in the mind you were born with—only the Buddha-mind with its marvelous illuminative wisdom that enlightens all things. Firmly believing in this and being free of all attachment whatsoever . . . that is known as the "believing mind."

A monk from the city of Sendai in northern Japan: What kind of preparation must we undergo to enable us to conform with this primary mind?

Bankei: There is no "primary mind" apart from what is seeking the answer to that question right now. The primary mind, detached from thought, has a perfect clarity that is directly conversant with all things. As evidence of this, couldn't you answer me without engaging in discrimination if I asked you something about Sendai?

A visiting monk: What happens when someone who believes in the Unborn dies, and the four elements of his physical body disperse? Is he born again or not?

Bankei: At the place of the Unborn, there's no distinction between being born and not being born.

A layman: When my mind was bothered by disordered thoughts last year, and I asked you how to deal with them, you told me to just let them come and go of themselves. I've done my best to follow that advice, but I've found it almost impossible to do.

Bankei: It's difficult because you have the idea that there is some method that will make your thoughts arise and cease of themselves.

Bankei to an assembly: It's essential that you people learn about the living Buddha-mind that functions vitally as you live and work. For hundreds of years now, the Zen teaching in both China and Japan has been mistaken. People have thought, and still do, that enlightenment is attained by doing zazen. They've tried to discover the "master of seeing and hearing."[2] They're dead wrong. *Zazen* is another name for the primary mind. It signifies peaceful sitting. A peaceful mind. When sitting, it just sits. When doing *kinhin*, it just walks. There's no way in the world anyone could preach the Buddhist Dharma, not even if he had all heaven and earth for a mouth. Those who attempt to preach it only end up blinding others. There wasn't a speck of trouble or illusion in the mind your mother gave you when she brought you into the world. From ignorance of this, you say something like, "I'm deluded because I'm an ordinary, unenlightened man," unfairly pushing the blame onto your parents. The Buddhas of the past and people of the present are one and the same substance—there is nothing setting them apart. It's like taking water from a river and pouring it into buckets of different shapes and sizes; when the weather turns cold and it freezes solid, the shape it takes, large, small, square, or round, varies according to the shape of the bucket you put it in. But thawed, it's all the same river water.

You don't know that you're already living Buddhas in all that you do. You think that you attain enlightenment and become a Buddha by piling up merit through religious practice. But since that's totally wrong, you go along pathetically, leaving one darkness only to enter another.

As for me, I don't preach about the Buddhist teaching. I only point out the false notions you bring with you.

Bankei's disciple Jōzen:[3] I'm greatly troubled about death. That's the reason I come here so often to see you. Surely, no matter could be more important to a human being.

Bankei: That very mind is the origin of Buddhist practice. Since you've been able to realize that much, if you don't turn from your purpose, you'll soon conform to the Way.

Jōzen: Just what does the expression "becoming a Buddha" mean?

Bankei: When you take what I tell you and make it your own, so that you haven't the slightest doubt about it, right at that moment you become a Buddha.

Bankei to an assembly: It's wrong for you to breed a second mind on top of the mind you already have by trying to *become* the Unborn. You're unborn right from the start. Many people talk about the "fundamental principle" of the Unborn, but there's nothing like that in the Unborn. If the Unborn had any principle at all, it wouldn't be unborn. There's no need for you to become the Unborn. The true Unborn has nothing to do with fundamental principles, and it's beyond becoming or attaining. It's simply *being as you are.*

A visiting monk: I have been practicing to achieve enlightenment. What about that?

Bankei: Enlightenment is something that stands in contrast to illusion. As each person is a Buddha-body just as he is, he hasn't a speck of illusion in him. What is it, then, that you want to enlighten?

The monk: But master, that would mean living life as an utter fool. Look at Bodhidharma. Look at all the Zen masters after him. They realized the great Dharma by attaining enlightenment.

Bankei: It is as just such a fool that a Tathagata saves people from suffering. Neither coming nor going, being just as you are at the time when you are born, without obscuring your mind—that's the very meaning of Tathagata! All the patriarchs of the past were exactly the same as that.

Once when Bankei was staying at the Kannon Hall at Kiyotani in Iyo Province, Kantarō, the head of a village named Utsu in that district, came to him regularly for Zen study. Although Kantarō probed and questioned searchingly, it was impossible for him to approach the master's lofty heights. One day while on his way to Kiyotani with a friend named Yoshino Yojizaemon, Kantarō said, "Every time I go there the master examines me with the same phrase, 'Has Kantarō come?' Wait and see, it will be the same today. But this time, when he says, 'Has Kantarō come?' I'm going to say, 'Who says that?' " When the two men reached Kiyotani, Bankei came out and greeted Yoshino. He said nothing to Kantarō. Finally, after a long pause, Kantarō said, "Well, master, how have you been?" Bankei said, "Who says that?" Taken completely aback, Kantarō bowed sheepishly.

At Aboshi,[4] a fellow named Hachirōbe said: I'm a follower of the Ikkō sect.[5] We place single-minded trust in Amida Buddha and say the Nembutsu in thanks for the salvation that Amida has assured us.

Bankei: But it seems to me that someone who calls on Amida's help while he's gambling and doing a lot of other things he shouldn't is just trying to put one over on Amida.

Since Hachirōbe had in fact been spending most of his time at the gambling mats, Bankei's remarks made a deep impression on everyone present.

Hachirōbe (on another occasion): Buddhist teachers of old worked many wonderful miracles. Can you work miracles, master?

Bankei: What sort of thing do you mean?

Hachirōbe: When the founder of the Ikkō sect was in Echigo, he had someone take a piece of paper across to the far side of a river. Standing on the opposite bank, he pointed a writing brush at it and the six characters of Amida's holy name appeared on the paper. People call it the Kawagoe Myōgō, and hold it in great reverence.[6]

Bankei (laughing): Magicians perform greater feats than

that. To mention people of that sort here at the place of the true Dharma would be like trying to compare dogs or cats with men.

A party of monks came to stay at the temple. After meeting with Bankei, each of them gave his understanding of the Dharma. There was one, however, who offered no opinion. "What about you?" asked Bankei.

He answered, "When I'm cold I put on some more clothes. When I'm hungry, I eat. When I get thirsty, I have something to drink. That's all there is."

"Well, then," said Bankei, "can you look at the others here and tell the depth of their understanding?"

"I can," replied the monk.

"Then tell me about the people next to you there. How do you size them up?"

"Why don't you say something about me personally?" the monk asked.

"Every word we've spoken has been about you," said Bankei.

A visiting monk stepped forward, saying, "This is not being, nonbeing, or emptiness."

"Right now where is 'this'?" asked Bankei.

Confused and wordless, the monk left.

A layman: For years now, I've been reading the teachings of the ancient masters, seeking earnestly to find out "Who is the master of seeing and hearing?" But to this day, I've been unable to discover who he is. How should I practice so that I can meet this master of seeing and hearing?

Bankei: I belong to the Buddha-mind sect. The "master of

seeing and hearing" and the person seeking him are not two. If you look for him outside yourself, you could go over the whole world seeking him and still never find him. The one unborn mind is the master in every man. When you see things with your eyes and hear things with your ears—when any of the six senses encounters an object of sense—this "master" is fully revealed in those acts.

A woman: I'm scared to death of thunder. Whenever I hear the sound of it I grow faint. My face turns pale. I'm almost paralyzed with terror. Please, master, tell me how to overcome this awful fear.

Bankei: When you were born, all you had was the unborn Buddha-mind. There wasn't any fear. Your fear is an illusion or figment of thought that you have created on your own after you came into the world. Thunder brings us rain; it's beneficial to us, not harmful. Your fear is not the result of anything that lies outside yourself. It's a trick that's played on you by that figment of thought. From now on, whenever you hear thunder, just trust single-mindedly in your own Buddha-mind, your own Buddhahood.

A visiting monk: Is there any merit in doing zazen?

Bankei: You shouldn't have a dislike for doing zazen, just as you shouldn't avoid chanting sutras, bowing, or anything else of that kind. Tokusan wielded a staff. Rinzai shouted Khat! Gutei held up one finger.[7] Bodhidharma sat facing a wall. Each was different, and yet all were measures used in response to an occasion present at a certain time. They were the expedient means of good and able masters. Intrinsically, there is no definitely established Dharma. If you try to give the Dharma a fixed interpretation, you merely blind your own eye. Just believe what I tell you with an open heart, and stay with what you were born with. Don't clutter up your mind thinking about the conditions of this and the probable effects of that. Be just like a mirror reflecting things. If you are, then have no doubt about it, there is no way you can avoid holding full and clear intercourse with all things.

A Zen monk from the Tamba area: I'm determined to become a Buddha at this meeting. I desire only to become a good person. Please, master, give me your instruction.

Bankei: You've come a long way to see me. Your aspirations are admirable. But they are all illusions. Your primary mind has absolutely no illusions, no desires or aspirations whatsoever. It straightens everything out, without desires and without hopes, by means of its illuminative wisdom. The idea of wanting to hasten on Buddhahood causes trouble too. But if you realize that you yourself create those hopes, if you stay with what you were born with and don't set yourself into confrontation with things, then your primary being reveals itself in its true form.

A layman: What happens when you become a Buddha? Where do you go?

Bankei: When you become a Buddha, there isn't any place to go. You're already everywhere, reaching even beyond the universe itself. If, on the other hand, you become something else, there are indeed plenty of places for you to go.

Bankei: There aren't any set objectives in my Dharma, as there are everywhere else. There's nothing set up to be enlightened about. There is no commenting on koans, no depending on what some Buddha or patriarch has said. There is only "direct pointing."[8] Since there is nothing to grasp, people can't come to terms with it easily. It's the people with intelligence and learning who have the greatest difficulty affirming it. They are hindered by what they know and by their inclination to use their minds. Illiterate people, on the other hand, ordinary womenfolk, for example, since they don't have this intellectual ability, may not be acclaimed by others and put forward as Zen masters, yet many of them penetrate to an unquestionably firm conviction. They go straight ahead in unswerving affirmation.

Though no one can make my Dharma entirely his own, it is like a lump of gold that is broken up and scattered about: For those who get one piece, there's one piece of brightness; for those who get two pieces, there are two pieces of brightness. Whether you can obtain one piece or two pieces or more, you never fail to profit in proportion to the amount you get.

A layman: Master, I've heard that you can see right into people's minds. Right now, what am I thinking?

Bankei: You're thinking that.

A priest named Kanrei Zogen: The Pure Land schools teach that we attain birth in the Pure Land "a hundred billion *koti* of Buddha-lands to the west." But they also say that it is "not far away."[9] Both are clearly the Buddha's preaching. Which is right? I think this is something a great many lay believers have doubts about.

Bankei: It is thanks to that difference that the true meaning is made clear.

Kanrei: Do the hundred billion *koti* of Buddha-lands represent an expedient teaching?[10]

Bankei: No, it's not an expedient teaching.

Kanrei: How is that?

146

Bankei: You might bring a crying child back into good humor by holding out an empty fist pretending there is something in it—that's a direct preaching for a little child.

A woman: I've heard that women have great difficulty attaining Buddhahood because of their deep karma. Is that true?

Bankei: When do you become a woman?

A woman: Women are said to have deep karma. We aren't allowed to climb sacred mountains such as Mount Kōya and Mount Hiei.[11] Their precincts are closed to women.

Bankei: There's a nunnery in Kamakura. It's closed to men.

A layman: When I hear unexpected noises such as the sound of a thunderclap, it sometimes startles me. I think it must be because my mind normally isn't really at ease. How can I keep myself from being startled no matter what happens?

Bankei: When something startles you, it's best just to be startled. If you try to keep yourself from being startled, your mind becomes two.

A monk: Tokusan had his staff. Rinzai had his shout. Good Zen masters of the past all used the staff and the shout. You don't use either, master. Why?

Bankei: Tokusan knew the use of the staff. Rinzai knew the use of the shout. I'm able to use my tongue.

A monk: Great priests such as Engo and Daie gave koans to their students to instruct them.[12] You never use any. Why is that?

Bankei: Did the Zen teachers who lived prior to Engo and Daie also use koans?

———

A monk: A Zen master of the past has said that great enlightenment proceeds from great doubt.[13] You don't utilize this great doubt in your teaching. Why?

Bankei: Long ago, when Nangaku went to the sixth patriarch and was asked, "What is this that thus comes?" he was totally bewildered. His doubts about it lasted for eight years.[14] Then he was able to give the reply, "The moment I said it was 'this' I'd miss the mark completely." Now, that's really great doubt and great enlightenment. Suppose you lost your only surplice, the one you were given when you became a monk, and you were unable to find it no matter how hard you looked for it. You'd search and search without letup. You'd be unable to stop searching for even an instant. That would be real doubt. People nowadays say that they need to have doubt because people in the past did. So they cultivate a doubt. But that's merely an imitation of a doubt, not a real one, so the day never comes when they arrive at a real resolution. It's as if you were to go off looking for something you hadn't really lost, pretending you had.

[Itsuzan]: Is it helpful for students to look through the Buddhist sutras and Zen records?

Bankei: There's a time for reading the Zen records. If you read them or the sutras while you're still seeking the meaning contained in them, you'll only blind yourself. When you read them after having transcended that meaning, they become proof of your attainment.

One winter when Bankei was preaching during a retreat at the Sanyū-ji in Bizen Province, laity and priests from Bizen and Bitchū assembled in great numbers to hear him.[15] At a place called Niwase, in Bitchū, there was a large temple of the

Nichiren sect, whose head priest was a learned cleric deeply venerated by his congregation.[16] At that time, Bankei's name was already known far and wide, and his teaching inspired great respect, so the Nichiren priest's followers all attended the meetings. Resenting this, the priest told them, "I've heard that Bankei isn't really enlightened. If I went there, I could give him a question I know he couldn't answer. I could stop him with a single word."

So saying, he showed up at one of the meetings. Standing at the rear of the assembly, in the middle of Bankei's talk he said in a loud voice, "The people here all listen to your talk and believe what you tell them. But someone like myself could never be expected to agree with the essential idea of your teaching. How can you save me when I don't accept your teaching?"

Bankei raised his fan and said, "Would you move forward here a little?"

The priest moved forward.

"Please come forward a bit more," said Bankei.

The priest advanced again.

"Look how well you accept it!" said Bankei.

The priest withdrew stupidly without saying another word.

Bankei (while we were having tea): One day, years ago, when I was studying under Zen master Dōsha, an attendant of Dōsha's named Zentei was discussing the Dharma with several other monks.

Zentei quoted some words that appear at the beginning of the *Blue Cliff Records:* "Prince Chang is clearly painted on the paper, but no matter how loudly you call out to him, he gives no answer."[17]

He then declared that each of us should try to answer in

place of Prince Chang. I was sitting close to him. He motioned to me, "Try to give an answer in Prince Chang's place," he said. Before the words had even left his lips, I struck him a blow with my hand. "Anyone could have done that," he said. "Try to answer with your mouth."

"*Yah!* You're lucky I didn't answer with my foot," I told him. He was completely thrown for a loss.

Once I [Itsuzan] asked: "Master, I've studied under you for a long time now. I've been privileged to serve as your attendant for several years. I think I can say that I've no doubts at all now about the essentials of the Dharma. But being by your side and seeing you like this, you are still a wonder to me: 'The deeper I penetrate, the firmer it is, the further I seek, the higher it gets.'[18] All I can ever do is heave a heavy sigh. Your great freedom in responding to those who come to see you seems to have no limits. It's like being on a ladder, unable to reach the sun and moon. How can one arrive at that complete attainment?"

The master said, "On the whole, Zen students can reach seven or eight parts out of a total ten. There are two or three they can't get past."

"How does one get past them?" I asked.

"There is no way," said the master.

"They haven't reached complete attainment, and there is no way that they can. . . . Where does the fault lie?"

The master was silent for a moment. Then he said, "It's because, after all, their aspiration in the great Dharma is not strong enough."

A monk: I've been working on the "Have no illusions!" koan for thirty years.[19]

Bankei: Say something about "Have no illusions!" just as you are right now!

The monk: Yesterday it rained.

Bankei coughed.

The monk: Today is clear.

Bankei struck him.

A nun from Izumo asked: Both of my parents are alive. How should I fulfill my duty toward them?

Bankei: You are being truly filial when you live in the Buddha-mind that you received from your parents when you were born. Filial piety consists of nothing else. You're being unfilial when you don't live in the unborn Buddha-mind.

Bankei to his disciples: When I was twenty-six and had my realization of the fundamental truth of the Unborn in that small hut at Harima, I went to Dōsha, and he confirmed it for me. Now, in point of its fundamental truth, there's not the slightest bit of difference between the understanding I had then and my understanding now. Yet with the perfection and clarity of my Dharma eye, I now have a total freedom that is fully conversant with the great Dharma. There is a difference of heaven and earth between the way I was then, when I was with Dōsha, and the way I am now. None of you here should doubt that the same thing will happen to you. You can be sure that the day will come when your Dharma eye will come to full perfection too.

Someone asked: Does it happen at a certain point, all at once?

Bankei: No, there is no certain time. When the eye of the Way becomes clear and bright, without a single imperfection of any kind, then it is perfect and complete. It comes as a result of cultivating it with total, unswerving devotion.

A man asked a question about the words and phrases of eminent Zen figures of the past.

Bankei: Once you understand one of those phrases, you then set about doubting another one. You could go on and work your way through a million such phrases and never have an end of it. If you listen closely to what I say and realize it for yourself, then those wonderful words and marvelous phrases will all be coming out of your own mouth. Unless that happens, what's the good of practicing the Way?

Bankei to his disciples: The people studying Zen nowadays spend all their time on old Zen words and stories, quoting this fellow and citing that one as they deliberate fruitlessly over their koans. Trailing doggedly after other people's words. Feeding on their dregs. Caught in another man's tub, unable to break out into real freedom. They're down in the dark caves, living with the disembodied spirits. You won't find any of those musers or cogitaters around here. Here, I make people stand absolutely alone and independent right from the start, with their eyes fully open, so they can reach out through all the universe. Each one of the words and sayings uttered by the worthy teachers of the past was given in response to a particular occasion, according to changing conditions—they were trying to stop a child's crying by showing him an empty hand. How could anyone who belongs to the family of Zen have even a single Dharma to preach! If you chase after phrases and get muddled up in words, you're no better off than a man who loses his sword over the side of a ship and then marks the spot where it fell in on the railing.

During the retreat of 1684 at the Kōrin-ji, I [Itsuzan] had an enlightenment experience one morning at dawn in the Zen hall. I went to the master for a personal interview and said, "Until now, I trusted implicitly in what you have taught us. I was deceived by your words. But now, today, I have attained a full and direct understanding of the matter of my self, without any reliance on your teachings. Yet everything is just as you have been telling us every day. It is impossible to put it into words."

"You don't have to," Bankei said. "I know all about it."

I said, "You have always said that there is no final great enlightenment. But from where I stand today, I can see that the only way that the Dharma can be known is for each person to grasp it for himself. When Rinzai was in Ōbaku's assembly, he asked three times about the essence of the Buddha Dharma, and each time he was struck by Ōbaku, without coming to any realization. But when he visited Daigu, and Daigu spoke a single word to him, he had a satori and said, 'There isn't much to this Buddha Dharma of Ōbaku's.' That was Rinzai's self-understanding."[20]

Bankei said, "Because they are ancient masters, you feel that there is something special about them. But they are no different from people today. Rinzai's satori at the hands of Daigu was his entrance into enlightenment. All true practicers, whether they lived in the past or whether they live today, experience such an entrance. But if you stop there, you content yourself with a small attainment. Unless you are very careful after you experience the first satori, it is extremely difficult for you fully to perfect your Dharma eye."

I replied, "I certainly do not question what you say. But right now, I have not a shadow of doubt about the Dharma.

There is no way I could possibly acquire any greater strength than I have right at this moment."

Bankei said, "It is easy to reach the place where you are now. To be free of doubt. To have no more questions. But the Dharma is unfathomably deep. The Buddha-wisdom is unfathomably profound. The further you penetrate, the deeper it is. It's for that reason I have never in my life been able to bring myself to speak a few words and confirm great enlightenment in someone. I think about their future and the path that lies before them."

In the fifth year of Genroku (1692), Bankei had gone into seclusion at the Jizō-ji in Kyoto to convalesce from a recurrence of his chronic illness. His disciple Sekimon, the head priest at the Ryūmon-ji, sent a monk named Tenkyū to Kyoto to see how the master was getting on. Tenkyū inquired about Bankei's health and then told him about some young monks at the Ryūmon-ji whose rough behavior and disrespect for the senior priests were disrupting the teaching in the training halls. He said that Sekimon wanted Bankei's permission to send them somewhere else, the Nyohō-ji on Shikoku or the Kōrin-ji in Edo, which, he thought, might bring about a change in their attitudes.

Bankei immediately summoned his attendants Shūin, Soryō, and Sonin, informed them of Sekimon's request, and then delivered the following stern rebuke: "The training hall of a monastery is constructed in order to gather together as many as possible of just such miscreants, deal with them, and make them into good men. Without considering that, and without a speck of compassion, Sekimon wants to get them off his hands and let them stir up their trouble somewhere else. How can he call himself a temple master? If men devoid of benevolence and compassion rise to positions as head priests, then my Dharma is as good as finished."

All of Bankei's disciples, both those who had become head priests and those who served as his attendants, were very reluctant to mention disorderly behavior in their monks in the master's presence. [*Ryakki*]

Among the people who arrived at the Ryūmon-ji for the great retreat was a monk from Mino who had a reputation as a thief. He had been the cause of trouble in temples and monasteries throughout the country. Seven or eight other monks from the Mino area, who were aware of the man's notoriety, went to the priest in charge of the retreat and said, "Everyone knows about that fellow. Just give the word, we'll see to it that he leaves here. We want to prevent him from having a chance to cause any disturbance during the retreat."

The priest reported the matter to the head priest, Sekimon, who in turn took it up with Bankei. Bankei's brow darkened. "Why do you think I've been asked to hold this retreat? I want each person who attends to realize his inherent wisdom. I want the evil to turn from evil and the good to continue being good. Now you want to let in only the honest and upright people and shut out all the bad. That is completely counter to all that I'm trying to do."

Sekimon said nothing, but he was deeply ashamed of having failed to understand Bankei's intention. [*Ryakki*]

There was a blind man in the city of Himeji who was able to tell peoples' thoughts and foresee their futures merely by hearing their voices. Once, a man was walking in the street outside his house singing a song. "He sings quite well for a headless man," the blind man remarked to his wife and servants. They just smiled at each other and attributed the remark to an old man's foolishness. "A man's mouth is in his head," they said. "He can't sing without that." "Wait and you shall see," he replied. Shortly afterward, the same man came back along the street singing as before. Suddenly, there was a terrible scream. It was followed by the sound of a head being severed from a body and a heavy object falling to the ground. Rushing outside, the servants found a headless, blood-covered body lying on the street. The swordsman who had done the deed explained to them that he had been following the man, waiting for a chance to kill him, in order to avenge his master's death. "I was about to strike him a short while before," he said, "but I decided to wait until he returned."

Observing that human nature was the same everywhere, the blind man said, "Even when people are extending words of congratulations to others, there is always a note of sadness hidden in their voices. And an edge of gladness always colors even their most solemn words of condolence. But master Bankei is different. When I hear his voice, whether he is praising or censuring, whether the circumstances are favorable or unfavorable, whether he is speaking to the high or to the low, the young or the old, the sound is always the same. It never fluctuates. It is always perfectly calm and even." [*Itsujijō*]

Bankei traveled to the Shōgen-ji in Mino Province for a ceremony in honor of the founder of the temple, the "National Teacher" Kanzan.[22] The abbot and the monks asked him to give a talk, but Bankei declined, saying that he felt too deep a veneration for Kanzan to speak in the same training hall where he had taught. Despite his firm refusal, the persistent entreaties of the abbot forced him at last to relent. It is said that the abbot had a chair brought out for Bankei to sit on but that he did not use it and spoke while sitting on the floor. Those who truly understand the Buddha Dharma are filled with profound respect for it. [*Seppō*]

During the great retreat of 1690, there was a report that someone had lost some money at the Fudō Hall. When Bankei took the teaching seat, a monk came forward and said, "I am a disciple of priest so-and-so at such and such temple. I have been practicing during this retreat in the Fudō Hall. The monk who sits next to me discovered some of his traveling money had disappeared. Since my seat was next to his, people suspected me. Please, master, would you have the matter investigated?"

"You didn't take it?" asked Bankei.

The monk said, "At such an unprecedented assembly as this? How could you suggest that I would commit such a shameless act?"

"All right," said Bankei.

"Unless the matter is cleared up," the monk went on, "this baseless accusation will follow me wherever I go. I'll have trouble being admitted to any religious gathering in the country. Please, master, I'm counting on you to help me."

"If we decide to look into the matter, I am certain we can find out who the guilty party is. Are you sure you want that?" said Bankei.

Suddenly the monk began to weep. "To do such a thing while listening to you preach the great Dharma every day. The shame I feel for my self-centered partiality is beyond words," he sobbed. [*Ryakki*]

Once, while Bankei was in Iyo Province at the Sairyō-ji, he encountered a leper and had occasion to admonish him. The leper took Bankei's words to heart. That night he asked the master to give him the tonsure and make him a monk. Bankei took up his razor and began shaving the leper's head. A retainer of Bankei's lay disciple Lord Katō named Machida Denzaemon was with Bankei at the time. He stared intently as Bankei, touching the leper's festering sores, performed the ceremony to completion. He did nothing to conceal the deep disgust he felt for the beggar, and when Bankei had finished, he quickly brought some water for him to wash his hands in. Bankei refused the water. "Your loathing mind is a lot filthier than that leper," he said.

Previous to that, when he was staying at the Gyokuryū-ji in Mino, a group of a dozen lepers came to see him. While the other priests tried their best to avoid the visitors, Bankei gave each of them some rice to eat out of his own bowl. His companions were profoundly ashamed. [*Ryakki*]

Once, Jikō-in, the wife of Lord Katō, sent two small eggplants, the first of the season, to the Nyohō-ji, where Bankei was staying. Since there was not enough to divide among the entire brotherhood, Sotetsu, the monk in charge of the kitchen, cooked them and served them in Bankei's soup. Later in the day, Bankei said, "What happened to those eggplants that were sent over from the castle?"

When Sotetsu told him what he had done, Bankei said, "You fed me poison."

He refused to eat any food for several days. [*Ryakki*]

Once, while eating a meal at the Jizō-ji in Yamashina, Bankei remarked how good the food tasted.

"The cook did an excellent job today," he said.

The young monk attending him said, "The master's portion was selected specially from the cooking pot."

"Who did the serving?" asked Bankei.

"Sokyō did," he replied.[23]

"It was shameful," said Bankei. "His discrimination extends even into the cooking pots."

From that time on, Bankei stopped eating the side dish of vegetables and took only rice. Sokyō, taking the master's admonition to heart, did the same. This continued for several months, until Bankei learned that Sokyō was not eating the side dish, and began eating it again. [*Ryakki*]

NOTES TO THE DIALOGUES

1. The passage Bankei cites from the *Heart Sutra* is: "O Shariputra, all things are empty appearances; they are unborn, undying."

2. This seems to have been a widely used koan in Bankei's day.

3. Tōgaku Jōzen (d. 1726).

4. Bankei's principal temple. See Introduction, p. 19.

5. Ikkō is the name by which the Jōdo-shin sect of Pure Land Buddhism used to be known. The Jōdo-shin sect teaches that the words "Namu-Amida-Butsu" ("I take refuge in Amida Buddha") should be called not with any purpose or end in mind but simply as thanks for Amida's "favor" or "gift" of salvation. Even a single calling, if uttered in complete sincerity, assures the devotee rebirth in Amida's Pure Land of Bliss. All other callings are done in thanks for the unconditional gift of salvation given by Amida to all sentient beings.

6. Shinran (1173–1262), founder of the Jōdo-shin sect, spent over four years in exile in Echigo Province. The six characters of Amida's name, or Myōgō (literally, "wonderful name"), are Na-mu-A-mi-da-Butsu. Kawagoe Myōgō means literally "the marvelous river-crossing name of Amida."

7. Bankei refers to Zen masters Tokusan Senkan (Te-shan Hsuan-

chien in Chinese; 782–865) and Rinzai Gigen (Lin-chi I-hsuan; d. 867). "Tokusan's staff" and "Rinzai's shout" are bywords in Zen. Gutei (Chu-chih; n.d.) is known for his "one-finger Zen." He answered all question-ers by raising one finger. See *Zen Comments on the Mumonkan*, case 3, pp. 43–49.

8. Bankei refers to the Zen maxim "You must see into your own na-ture and attain Buddhahood by directly pointing to the mind."

9. Nothing else is known of Kanrei Zogen: the statements he men-tions appear in two sutras that the Pure Land Jōdō-shin sect regards as its scriptural authority; the first is in the *Amida Sutra*, the second, the *Meditation Sutra*. A *koti* is a very large number, explained variously as a hundred or a thousand million.

10. Generally speaking, the term "expedient (or skillful) means" is used to refer to a teacher adapting his teaching to the capability of his students, guiding them by using methods that are not, strictly speaking, a direct expression of ultimate truth.

11. Mount Kōya, in present Wakayama prefecture, and Mount Hiei, northeast of the city of Kyoto, are the two great mountain monasteries of Japan. The nunnery referred to is the Tōkei-ji, popularly known as the "divorce temple," adjacent to the Engaku-ji in Kamakura.

12. Engo Kokugon (Yuan-wu K'o-ch'in in Chinese; 1083–1135) and Daie Sōkō (Ta-hui Tsung-kao; 1089–1163) were two great masters of the Lin-chi Zen sect during the Sung dynasty, when the koan system, with which they are closely associated, began to develop. Engo was the com-piler and joint author of the *Hekiganroku* koan collection, and Daie was his most important disciple.

13. This well-known Zen saying was first spoken by the master Meng-shan Te-i (Mōsan Tokui in Japanese; 1231–?) of the late Sung dynasty. For the term "great doubt," or "great ball of doubt," see Notes to the Dharma Talks, number 28.

14. Enō (Hui-neng in Chinese; 638–713), the sixth patriarch of Zen in China, uttered these words to Nangaku Ejō (Nan-yueh Huai-jang;

677–744); they later came to be used as a koan. When Nangaku was asked this question, he was unable to answer it. He went off and concentrated on it for eight years and finally was able to give this reply.

15. The Sanyū-ji was the temple of Bokuō Sogyū (d. 1695), the Dharma heir of Bankei's teacher Umpo Zenjō. See Introduction. Bizen and Bitchū are old provinces in present Okayama prefecture.

16. The Nichiren, or Hoke (Lotus), sect was founded by Nichiren (1222–1282).

17. The *Hekiganroku* (see note 12), compiled and partly authored by Engo Kokugon, is one of the most important Zen koan collections. Soon after it was first printed, however, Engo's successor, Daie Sōkō, decided that its circulation would be detrimental to true Zen study; he had copies of the work destroyed and the woodblocks from which it had been printed burned. More than 150 years later, the text was recompiled and reprinted. The words Zentei quotes here are found not in the *Hekiganroku* itself but in one of its prefaces, written by one Sankyō Rōjin (San-chiao Lao-jen in Chinese), who tells of the reasons for Daie's action. He writes of the risk in republishing the work that readers will "take the finger pointing to the moon for the moon itself." Then he says, "In a poem inscribed on the portrait of a man of the past [Prince Chang], it is written that 'Prince Chang is clearly revealed here on the paper, but you can raise your voice and call out to him all you like, there won't be any answer.' Anyone who wants to contemplate this book must first penetrate these words."

18. Confucius's disciple Yen Hui said with a deep sigh, "The more I aspire to it, the higher it soars. The deeper I penetrate, the harder it becomes. I see it in front, but suddenly it is behind. Step by step the Master [Confucius] skillfully lures one on. . . . Even if I wanted to stop, I could not. Just when I feel that I have exhausted every resource, something seems to rise up, standing out sharp and clear. Yet though I long to pursue it, I can find no way of getting to it at all." Confucian *Analects*, 9, 10.

19. "Have no illusions" (in Japanese, *Makumōzō*): This Zen expression figures in a number of stories and dialogues in Zen literature. It is unclear to which of these the priest is referring. The T'ang master Mugō (Wu-yeh in Chinese) is said to have responded with these words whenever students asked him questions. Also, in a dialogue between Zen master Ch'ang-sha and the minister Chu, the minister said, "An earthworm is cut in two. Both parts move. Which contains the Buddhanature?" Ch'ang-sha replied, "Have no illusions!" *Dentō-roku, ch.* 10.

20. Ōbaku Kiun (Huang-po Hsi-yun; d. ca. 850). This account is given in Sasaki, *The Record of Lin-chi*, p. 50.

21. The *Dainichi-kyō* (Sanskrit, *Mahavairochana Sutra*) is a fundamental text of the Japanese esoteric schools.

22. Kanzan Egen (1277–1360) was the founder of the Myōshin-ji in Kyoto. *Kokushi*, "National Teacher," is an honorary title awarded by imperial decree.

23. Dairyō Sokyō (1638–1688) was Bankei's chief disciple, heir, and successor at the Ryūmon-ji. Bankei seems to have loved him deeply and to have placed great hopes on him to carry on his teaching line. When Dairyō died, five years before Bankei, Bankei was deeply disappointed. He is reported to have said at the time: "I have lost both my arms."

Unnecessary Words

Unnecessary Words—Zeigo in Japanese—comprises seventy-three items. It contains a record of Bankei's talks and dialogues with his students and the Zen teachers and priests of other sects who came to him for interviews.

The editor, Sandō Chijō (1667–1749), was a priest in Bankei's teaching line who was twenty-six years old when Bankei died. In his introductory remarks below, Chijō states that he obtained the first part of Unnecessary Words *from a manuscript collection of Bankei's informal talks (*fusetsu) *that his teacher, Zen master Itsuzan, gave him. The rest of the work was apparently put together from other sources by Chijō himself.* (NW)

PREFACE BY SANDŌ CHIJŌ

The admiration and respect that men feel for their teacher's virtuous achievements arise in them naturally. Although they may be determined to remain silent about his wonderful words and deeds, they find themselves unable to refrain from speaking out. Hence these "unnecessary" words. With the master's death, a lifetime of meritorious deeds and unsurpassed utterances, countless in number, perished forever. Fewer than one in many thousands have survived. The task of assembling them has now become extremely difficult. In compiling this work, I have gathered together what I could—a leaf or two here, a few blades of grass there. Because of this, the entries are mixed randomly, and there are temporal and geographic discrepancies in the order of the events.

Long ago, in the T'ang dynasty, the great Chinese Zen master Ummon prohibited his disciples from recording his words. In spite of that, an attendant named On copied them down, and consequently they have been transmitted to the present day. His example is something we must deeply cherish and envy. While master Bankei was alive, he, too, expressly forbade his followers to transcribe his talks or dialogues. But in his case, there was no attendant On to jot them down on his paper robe; all those words, like exquisite music to the soul, were cast aside and remain uncollected—they were just left for the sparrows to play around with! What a grievous waste!

Some years after Bankei's death, his disciple Zen master Jōmyō [Itsuzan] showed me a manuscript in his possession— a transcript copy of one of the master's informal talks (*fusetsu*). I cleansed my hands and rinsed out my mouth to purify myself, and then I perused it reverently. As I read, I felt as if I were sitting before the master himself, listening intently to his compassionate preaching of the Dharma. I raised the manuscript to my head in veneration. Then I took out my brush and made a copy. This I placed carefully inside a box with other valuables, for what I had obtained was no mere costly gem! Alas, Zen master Jōmyō, Zen master Reigen, and priest Daikei Kakkō, who served many years as the master's attendants, were under strict orders never to record the words he spoke; and, owing to their deep respect for him, they could never bring themselves to disobey.[1] As a result, knowledge of his teaching has been virtually unobtainable. And so now, on the occasion of compiling this record of the master's sayings and doings, I took out my box and searched until I found the transcription I had made years before. How could anything surpass this treasure of the Dharma? I respectfully place it at the beginning of this collection of unnecessary words.

HOW COULD THE SCHOOL OF "DIRECT POINT-ing" have a single Dharma to preach to others?[2] You have only to address yourself to your original face—the one you got as you dropped from your mother's womb—to discern your own nose holes. Look at yourself! What do you lack as you see and hear amid the various circumstances of your daily life? You are perfectly all right just the way you are now. But when you let the slightest thought or inclination to do something arise in your mind, you go completely astray. When you are watching and listening, you are unborn. When you are not watching and listening, you are undying. This original un-bornness and deathlessness soars radiantly beyond past and present, its brightness transcending that of the sun or moon. It is immediately present in all things, its vastness encompass-ing heaven and earth. It far transcends the realms of illusion and enlightenment, totally detached from the domains of the enlightened and the unenlightened alike. In the Unborn, each and every thing is originally true and possessed of a mar-velously unhindered freedom. The utter incomprehensibility and perfect virtue of the Unborn are present at all times in the mind of each one of you and cannot be obtained anywhere else. People speak of the essential mind of the Buddhas and patriarchs, but there is not a hairbreadth of difference be-tween their minds and your mind right now. Yet you want to give rise to thoughts, to seek outside yourselves for Buddhahood, the Dharma, knowledge, emancipation. You create the very obstructions that hinder you and keep you from conforming to your original mind.

An old Buddha said: "The moment Yajñādatta ceased his crazed pursuit, he was enlightened."[3] Even were you to gain complete knowledge of all the sutras that the Buddha ever preached, and to understand all the intricacies of the Zen koans, and to display that understanding with confidence, when you look deeply and carefully, you will see that it is all so much external dust clinging to you like filth. When your final hour comes, the time for the dispersal of your four elements, none of that knowledge will be of any use to you. Much better to turn inwardly—into your own selves—to act directly and immediately using the vital, primal energy of the Unborn. What ingenious methods do you think the Buddha-patriarchs use when they appear in the world? They just pull out the nails, wrench free the wedges, in order to make you into emancipated, self-dependent people free of all attachments. Listening to me, you may think that you have grasped what I have just said. You may imagine that you really believe in it. But because your conviction is still incomplete, you are susceptible to being deluded by others, and so you live like disembodied spirits, clinging to trees and blades of grass, unable to gain complete freedom for yourselves. You lose your way under a bright cloudless sky, and you become someone else's man, mean and mediocre. Isn't that lamentable?

A radiance emanated from the master's eyes. It illuminated people and never failed to penetrate the hearts of those who came before him. He was like a bright mirror, comprehending with perfect clarity everything about them before they had said or done a single thing. "If a barbarian came before him, a barbarian was revealed. If a Chinese came before him, a Chinese was revealed."[4] Once, when he was at the Kōrin-ji in Edo, a monk came to him and made his bows.[5]

"Show me how you use the Dharma," Bankei said.

The monk set forth his understanding.

"Your words and your attainment do not match," said Bankei. "What you say flies before the soaring dragon. What you are hobbles behind a lame tortoise. Before you came, you discussed what you would say to me with a more advanced student. You thought you would be able to put something over on me. But when you come before a teacher who possesses the true Dharma eye, you can no more keep something from him than you could hide from the sun itself." The monk rose and prostrated himself penitently before Bankei in gratitude. He then received his teaching with great reverence.

During a conversation, the master remarked: "Where I am now is a realm the Buddha-patriarchs themselves could not fathom."

Bankei's decisiveness in executing everyday affairs was beyond understanding. When he engaged in some undertaking, the monks attending him thought at times that he was neglecting to do what he should be doing, or even doing the reverse. They simply could not explain his intentions. Later, however, they would discover their significance and fundamental truth.

The master was constantly using the word "Unborn" in his teaching. Those who came to him all benefited from it in proportion to their capacities, just like the fish, shellfish, turtles, and whales that inhabit the boundless ocean and are able to partake fully of its waters.

The master said: "The essence of our school is expressed in the saying 'If there is even a hairbreadth of difference, you are as far from it as heaven is from earth.'[6] At the instant in a Zen encounter when two minds move without separation, it is like two mirrors reflecting each other. Each and every thing is presented in true suchness. Each and every thing is completely true. There is nothing above to catch hold of and nothing below to support you. You live in your original perfection, unborn and undying, immersed in a samadhi of total freedom, where nothing, not even stone walls, can hinder you. You must realize that it is your own views and opinions that obstruct you and that 'doing nothing' is a dark, ghost-filled cave. It is no different with the words I am speaking to you now. You commit a fatal error if you seek some meaning in them. If I give you a word of explanation and you cling to it, you go hopelessly astray. It is best not to stop or abide anywhere. The words and phrases that I speak, the shouts from my mouth and the blows from my staff, are a ration of unchewable iron nails. You couldn't possibly get your teeth into them."

The master continually lamented the many evil habits and customs prevalent in the Zen training halls of the day. His own teaching was direct, determined solely by the situation at hand. He did not allow the indiscriminate use of the staff or the shout, nor did he permit students to engage in literary pastimes, dialogues, or other unnecessary displays of Zen activity. What is more, he pledged not to quote sayings from Buddhist or Zen records in his teachings. In responding to those who came to him, whoever they were and whatever their intellectual ability, he always used plain language. At the time, Zen training was tied inextricably to Chinese-style terms and phrases quoted from the Buddhist teachers of the past. But the master was able to make his students cut right through to the bone and marrow, spontaneously and naturally, by speaking to them in the informal, colloquial Japanese they used in their daily lives.

In the instruction of students under his charge, the master did not lay down any rules or establish any regulations. Yet a silent, respectful atmosphere always prevailed in his temples—an example of "Not governing, yet having no disorder; doing what is right without being told."

A layman asked: "Isn't what you say about the 'Unborn' similar to the teaching Layman Vimalakirti gave to Mahākātyāyana?"[7]

"Tell me what you mean," replied Bankei.

"Well, according to the sutra, Vimalakirti said, 'Mahākātyāyana, you must not use the activity of mind to preach the changeless reality of things. All things are fundamentally unborn and undying; that is the meaning of impermanence and suffering.' "

"Vimalakirti said that in order to instruct Mahākātyāyana," said Bankei. "My teaching is designed to make people penetrate directly what is beyond words."

A priest of the esoteric Shingon sect visited the master and said: "The principle of the Unborn in our school's meditation on the letter A contains the two gates of eliminating delusion and of actualizing fundamental reality.[8] Wouldn't the teaching you expound fall into the latter category?"

"Come closer," Bankei said.

The priest moved forward.

Raising his voice, Bankei shouted, "What aspect is that!"
The priest was struck dumb.
A monk in the audience stuck out his tongue.[9]

A monk said to Bankei: "When you read about the ancient
Zen worthies, you notice how they used many different words
in teaching their pupils, depending on the situation that con-
fronted them. Yet you use only the word 'Unborn.' Don't you
find that using just a single word hampers your exercise of the
Dharma?"

"You haven't read about Gutei?" Bankei said. "Whenever
someone asked Gutei a question, he held up a finger. He said,
'I have grasped the one-finger Zen of Tenryū. I can use it for a
lifetime yet never use it up.'[10] He didn't say a word, just raised
his finger. How can something that a man could not exhaust
in a lifetime hamper the exercise of the Dharma? And it is not
only Gutei's one-finger Zen. Rinzai's Khat! Tokusan's staff.
Mugō's 'No illusions!' Zuigan's 'Main character,' hitting the
ground, striking a drum—they are all cases of the great activity that every authentic Zen master possesses.[11] It isn't that the
word 'Unborn' does not exist in the Buddhist scriptures and
Zen records. It does. But since the time of the first Buddha-
patriarchs, who except for this old priest has used a single
word exclusively in teaching his students?"

The monk thanked Bankei penitently and thereafter became a devoted follower of his teaching.

The master said: "A Zen teacher cannot help others unless he
himself possesses the discerning Dharma eye. If he has fully
perfected his Dharma eye, he is able to know someone to the
very marrow merely by observing his face as he approaches.
He can know all about him merely by hearing his voice outside the temple walls. It is like a bright mirror, which reflects

fully and distinctly whatever faces it, revealing both the beautiful and the ugly. Each word he speaks, everything he does in dealing with students, strikes right to the place of their affliction like a sharp gimlet, dissolving their attachments, breaking off their shackles, ushering them into a realm of wonderful freedom and blissful joy. Unless he can do that, what help can he hope to be to others? It is in this essential point, the possession of the Dharma eye, that our school surpasses all others. We call it the 'treasure and eye of the right Dharma,' the 'special teaching apart from the scriptures,' the 'legacy of the Buddha-patriarchs.' Look at the Buddha-patriarchs who have appeared through the ages. They could all tell the black from the white in less time than it takes a spark to jump from a flint. They grasped the essentials with lightning speed. Could such men have lacked the Dharma eye? But Zen teachers of recent times erroneously regard a student's conversance with words and letters as the criterion by which to determine whether he has grasped the essence of Zen. They certify someone because he is quick and clever at the give-and-take of Zen dialogue. This burdens the student with a heavy yoke. Not only are such teachers mistaken themselves; they misguide others as well. You can no longer find a man capable of facing a person and clearly judging him before he has made a move or said a word. Such men have disappeared completely. What a terrible pity."

In recent years, the master has been converting people to his teaching of the unborn mind effortlessly. For the past three hundred years, teachers and students everywhere have been clinging to their practice, pursuing the strange and unusual, without attending to the efficacy of what they were doing. It has consequently been extremely difficult for a student to learn from his teacher's personal instruction. In the past, when master Bankei taught people, he would receive their questions and engage them in dialogues, but their responses could never match his. Most went to the edge of the precipice and then backed away. From Bankei's middle years, students began coming in tremendous numbers—gathering like storm clouds—in order to have interviews with him. They were devoted to him before they even saw his face. When they actually came before him, they emptied their minds and received his teaching in a state of complete selflessness. Now he does not even have to expend much effort on their instruction.

Once, when the master was at the Fumon-ji on the island of Hirado, the abbot of the Kōdai-ji in Nagasaki came to him for an interview.[12] After they had conversed for a while, the priest said, "The teaching you have expounded is clear and direct. One must cut off all illusions and passions at their source, without resorting to religious practice. But then what about that story of Zen master Chōkei wearing out seven sitting cushions doing zazen?"

"You misread those records," said Bankei. "Chōkei went to many masters, including Reiun, Seppō, and Gensha, over a period of twelve years—that is when he wore out those seven cushions.[13] But it still did not bring him understanding. Then one day, as he was raising a screen, he suddenly attained great enlightenment. He composed a verse: 'How different it is! How different it is! I raised up a screen and saw the whole world. If anyone asks me to explain what I have seen, I'll take my fly whisk and strike him on the mouth.' I think you had better take another look at that passage."

The priest could only nod his head in wonder.

The high-ranking Shingon priest Kōgen, head abbot of the Ninna-ji in Kyoto, visited Bankei at the Jizō-ji in Yamashina.[14]

After the exchange of greetings, Kōgen said, "I am an heir to the Shingon sect's esoteric teachings, but I am unable to penetrate their essential meaning. For example, in the 'Abiding Mind' chapter of the *Dainichi Sutra*, it says, 'Know the source of your own mind just as it is in its suchness.'[15] So far, all my efforts to discover the source of my own mind have been unsuccessful. Reading through the records of the Zen school, I have been deeply impressed by the severe, uncompromising methods that Zen teachers use in leading students to the truth. I want you to use your skillful means on me."

"There is only a very thin fabric separating you from your mind-source," said Bankei. "But 'if there is even a hairbreadth of difference, you are as far from it as heaven is from earth.' "[16]

A moment passed.

"What is obstructing you right now!" said Bankei.

Kōgen nodded in affirmation—then bowed in obeisance. After that, he was a frequent visitor at Jizō-ji.

Zen master Tenkei of the Sōtō school visited the master while he was at the Kōrin-ji in Edo.[17] After an exchange of greetings, Tenkei said: "Some years ago, when you stopped over at my temple in Shimada, I didn't know about your teaching. Later, when I learned about it, I realized how wrong I had been. Master, I now have the deepest respect for the marvelous working of your great Zen activity."

Tenkei was holding a fan. He raised it.

"What do you see, master? I see a fan."

Bankei just shook his head.

"The instruction is respectfully received," said Tenkei.

When Bankei was in his thirties, he often visited the village of Ikaruga in his home province of Harima. Although the villagers loved and respected him, Jakua, the head priest of the

Bussho-in, a Tendai temple in the village, was unwilling to accept Bankei, dismissing him as a young monk unworthy of notice.[18] Only the repeated urging of the villagers made Jakua at last relent and agree to meet Bankei.

Jakua began by casually putting some questions to Bankei, who answered them all with unsettling promptness and ease. Jakua then mustered all his learning and tried again and again to confound Bankei. At length, he had nothing left to ask.

He reflected to himself: I can certainly understand why master Saichō, the founder of our school, established three forms of teaching—Tendai, esotericism, and Zen—at the head temple on Mount Hiei.[19]

From then on, Jakua treated Bankei with the greatest respect and visited him frequently. Some years later, Jakua was invited to Kyoto to lecture on the sutras at the Enryaku-ji, the head Tendai temple on Mount Hiei. After accepting the invitation, he made a special trip to the Ryūmon-ji in Hamada to see Bankei. When he told Bankei of the invitation, Bankei raised a finger in the air and said: "*Jari!*[20] Can you lecture on this sutra?"

Jakua was dumbfounded. Cold sweat poured down his body. He sent word that very day to the Enryaku-ji, canceling the lecture. He then resigned his position as a Tendai priest and donned the robes of a Zen monk, becoming a disciple of Bankei's. He devoted himself to his practice with unfaltering diligence. People called him "the horned tiger of the Zen forest."[21] Known by the name Sengaku Soryū, he eventually became one of Bankei's Dharma heirs, but he died before Bankei.

Before he took the vows and became a Buddhist priest, the Zen master Shingetsu of the Ōbaku sect once visited the master at the Kōrin-ji in Edo.[22]

"How are you employing the Dharma?" Bankei asked.

"I have been reciting the *Lotus Sutra* for many years," said Shingetsu.

"Who recites the sutra?" asked Bankei.

"The one who pronounces the words," said Shingetsu.

"Who pronounces the words?" asked Bankei.

"Eyes horizontal. Nose vertical," replied Shingetsu.

"Don't give me that, you mealymouthed swindler!" barked Bankei. "Now tell me: *Who pronounces the words!*"

Shingetsu hesitated.

"If the teachers of our school do not possess the all-discerning Dharma eye, they can never become the teachers of men and gods," said Bankei. "Do you have a share of that eye?"

"Well, I believe I have my share of it," said Shingetsu.

"All right," said Bankei. "Can you give me an assessment of each person at this gathering?"

"There is no one here," said Shingetsu, looking around.

"Each and every person sitting here is distinguished by certain qualities," said Bankei. "Aren't you able to assess them?"

"Can you?" replied Shingetsu.

"If I couldn't, I might even blunder into approving someone like you," said Bankei.

Shingetsu's jaw dropped in amazement.

"There is no one in the entire country, or in China either, who could parry your Zen thrusts. I am certainly fortunate to have encountered you and had such a searching interview," said Shingetsu.

"No one but this old priest could have made you know the error of your ways," said Bankei. "Be diligent from now on. Your efforts will be rewarded."

Bankei was constantly teaching his monks about the Buddha-mind. One time, he said: "It is originally unborn and knows unmistakably the beautiful and the ugly without recourse to a single thought. It is just like knowing whether someone you meet is a stranger or an old friend. You don't resort to thought, but you know it with unmistakable clarity nonetheless—that is the marvelous wonder of the primary mind."

One of the monks said: "Granted that I know immediately if someone is an old friend or not, but thoughts still pass through my mind. Why is that?"

Bankei paused. Then, raising his voice, he shouted: "Originally, there are no thoughts!"

"I'm certain that thoughts occur!" the monk shouted back.

Without replying, Bankei made a long exhaling sound: *"Pfuu . . . pfuu . . ."*

The monk sat stupidly, confused and unsure. A few days later, he experienced a sudden satori, and went to Bankei for an interview. Bankei just smiled.

Once, after Bankei had given a talk at the Kōrin-ji, a samurai, proud of his skill in the fighting arts, approached him for an interview.

"I trained for many years in the art of dueling," he said. "When I had mastered it, my arms moved in perfect harmony with my mind. If I were to face an opponent now, my blade would split his skull before his weapon even moved. It's just like your possessing the Dharma eye."

"You say you have perfected your art," Bankei said. "Try to strike me."

The samurai hesitated.

"My blow has already fallen," said Bankei.

The man's jaw sagged. "I'm astonished," he said with a sigh. "Your stroke is swifter than the spark off a flint. My head rolls at my feet. Please, master, teach me the essentials of your Zen."

With each visit to the Kōrin-ji, the man's veneration for Bankei grew. While Bankei was in Edo, many swordsmen came to him for interviews. All of them encountered his powerful attack and became his devoted followers.

A monk asked Bankei: "How does 'fundamental purity and clarity' suddenly give rise to the mountains, rivers, and great earth?"[23]

"Whose mountains and rivers?" replied Bankei.

The monk could not answer.

At the great retreat of 1690, the Sōtō Zen master Gekkei was among the visiting priests.[24] They were quartered in the Chikurin-ken, which had been set aside as a guest residence for senior clerics. Gekkei went to the abbot's chambers for an interview with Bankei.

"My eye is just the same as yours," he declared.

Bankei blew out a breath.

Gekkei struck him.

"I'll take two or three of those," said Bankei.

"What are you doing talking about two and three?" said Gekkei.

"I've reeled you in with one cast of my line and tossed you down into the Double-Hoop Iron Mountains," Bankei said with a loud laugh.[25]

Gekkei made his bows and returned to the guest quarters. There he confessed to the other Zen masters what had happened. As he told them about the methods Bankei had used, they quaked uncontrollably with fear.

Bankei was an easy person for his attendants to serve. When I asked Itsuzan about this, he said: "One of the ancients said that it is easy to serve a superior man but extremely difficult to please him. That is just the way I found it. I served the master for years. I was always by his side. We were like a fish and water, each oblivious of the other's presence. It was never the slightest trouble for me; and yet I never knew him to be pleased with me. He was someone to look up to, to respect, but it was impossible to take liberties and be overly familiar with him.

"The master said that 'those who are able to associate closely with a true Buddhist teacher are indeed fortunate. No matter what they say or do, whether they are active or at rest, they are drawn deeper and deeper into the profundity of the teacher's enlightened mind.'

"When I was a young monk and hadn't yet penetrated to realization, I was unsure of those words about entering deeper into the master's mind. Much later, I came to know how true they were."

There were never any set methods or rules in the master's way of doing things. In the years after Bankei's death, when Zen master Itsuzan was residing at the Jizō-ji in Yamashina, he was visited by Zen master Kogetsu Zenzai.[26] Kogetsu asked him repeatedly about Bankei's daily behavior.

"The master's daily life was without rules or patterns of any kind," Itsuzan told him. "There was nothing at all out of the ordinary about him. He remained in a state of *buji*.[27] But in dealing with students, responding to changing circumstances, his limits were truly fathomless. It has never been seen before, not even among the ancients."

Kogetsu heaved a sigh of admiration.

In his early thirties, Bankei traveled to Kanazawa in Kaga Province to visit Zen master Tesshin at the Tentoku-in.[28] He stayed for several days. One night, Tesshin calmly said: "Do you remember that dialogue [we had] when we were studying with Dōsha? I'd like to go over it again."

"I see the spiritual tortoise still sweeps his tail through the mud," said Bankei with a smile.

Tesshin just laughed.

A monk named Sokan came for an interview. After several exchanges, Bankei said: "What you're holding up to me is something that comes after the appearance of the Awesome Sound King Buddha.[29] What I teach is prior to before and after. You can't raise it into thought."

Hearing this, Bankei's student Sotei suddenly shouted: "My immense debt to the Buddha-patriarchs is at last paid!"[30]

"The bystander got the greater part," said Bankei.

Once, Bankei was sitting with his attendants Sogaku, Shūin, and Sonin.[31]

"Are the fifty-two stages of bodhisattva practice all clearly defined?" asked Sonin.

"How could they be otherwise?" replied Sogaku.

Shūin nodded in agreement.

They appealed to Bankei, who said: "People who read sutras get caught in their web."

In his early thirties, Bankei was staying at the Sanyū-ji in Okayama, Bitchū Province. The provincial daimyo, Lord Ikeda, was a zealous champion of the doctrines of Wang Yang-ming. His infatuation with the neo-Confucian philosopher finally led him to begin expelling Buddhist priests from the province and destroying their temples.

Some priests stayed on and continued to teach by engaging in indiscriminate word games using Zen phrases. A group of these neo-Confucian samurai came to the Sanyū-ji to interrogate Bankei.

"You Zen people create refuges like this for yourselves," one of them said. "Then you ensconce yourselves in them and turn your backs on the world. When you do not succeed with reason and you run out of words, you beat people with your staffs and shout at them. Temples have become breeding grounds for a race of stubborn, parasitic frauds! We want you out of here!"

"When Confucianists fail to get their way with reason and run out of words, what do they do?" asked Bankei.

The samurai hesitated, not knowing what to say.

Bankei hit him with his staff. "Ah!" he remarked admiringly. "A truly life-giving staff."

Bankei's response came like the spark from a struck flint, leaving the samurai gasping for breath.

On his way back to Nagasaki in his thirty-third year, Bankei stopped for a few days at the Tafuku-ji in Bungo Province to visit Zen master Kengan Zen'etsu.[32] The two men took the opportunity to catch up. A layman had been coming to Kengan for several days and nights seeking help in understanding the koan about "perfect oneness whether sleeping or waking."[33] But as he was still no closer to grasping it, Kengan deferred to Bankei on the matter. Bankei called out to the layman and asked him to come forward. When he responded, Bankei said: "Is that sameness? Is it difference?"

The layman pressed his head to the ground in a deep bow, utterly convinced by the words Bankei had uttered.

Kengan sighed in admiration. "How swiftly he responds to the occasion."

Once when Bankei, in his mid-thirties, was residing at the Kaian-ji in his native village of Hamada, a messenger arrived from Lord Katō, the daimyo of Iyo Province. Bankei ordered his attendant Sokyō to peel a sheet of paper from a spot on the wall where he had previously pasted it.[34] Underneath was an inscription: *On such and such day, in such and such month, a messenger will arrive from Lord Katō*. Bankei had foreseen that the man would come and had known the exact date of his arrival. People were amazed. But it was not an isolated incident in Bankei's life; strange and unusual feats were common in his younger days. Later, however, he ceased to display such powers, fearing they might generate rumors that would be harmful to his students. From then on, there was nothing out of the ordinary in his behavior. To all appearances, his life was normal in every way.

In his early thirties, Bankei practiced at a hermitage in the mountains of Hitachi. During one of his visits there, he said to a monk who was staying with him: "It's unusually cold this winter. Old Umpo is advanced in years. I'm concerned about his health. Besides, last night in Osaka, the wife of my student Enni passed away. I received their kindness and charity for many years. I want to go and offer my condolences."

"I came here to share this hut and practice with you because I thought you were a man of the Way," the monk replied reproachingly, his face coloring. "Osaka is many days from here. There's no way you could know someone died there yesterday. Why do you try to pull such shameless tricks, you lying bonze!"

"If that's how you feel, then come along with me," said Bankei. "Then there won't be any doubt about it."

The two men set out for Osaka. When they arrived, the

monk said: "If it isn't true, I'm going to rip that priest's robe right off your back."

"Fine," said Bankei.

Arriving at the house, Bankei sent word to Enni, who hastened joyfully to the entrance to meet him.

"I had been hoping for several days that you would come," he said. "My wife passed away, and tomorrow is the ceremony in observance of the seventh day. Your presence here is an answer to my prayers."

Bankei glanced at his traveling companion. All trace of his former contempt had vanished.

"I promise to follow you for the rest of my life," he declared humbly.

Bankei then resumed his journey, but he arrived at Zuiō-ji to find that Umpo had died the previous night. After the funeral, he completed his mourning at the foot of Umpo's reliquary tower.

During the winter retreat of 1684 at the Kōrin-ji in Edo, Bankei's disciple Sonin was in the monks' hall reciting the *Diamond Sutra* one afternoon. When he came to the words "There is nothing, not the smallest Dharma, to obtain—that is called supreme perfect enlightenment," he experienced a sudden satori. Without knowing what he was doing, he cast aside his sutra book and proceeded to the abbot's chambers. As he attempted to express his realization to Bankei, he was trembling so badly he could not utter the words.

"I don't have to rely on your words," said Bankei. "I can see with my own eyes."

Sonin made three bows and retired.

A few days later, Sonin was attending Bankei. They began talking.

"You have always taught me that illusion and enlightenment do not exist," said Sonin. "But viewing matters from where I stand today, I believe that even the great Zen masters of the past must have reached a time when they penetrated to enlightenment."

"What this old priest tells you," said Bankei, "expresses the great matter just as it is in itself, without defiling it, without smearing it with mud. There is a time and place when each person grasps it. That is the way it has always been, throughout the past and present . . ."

Bankei addressed the assembly at Nyohō-ji:[35] "All of you have been blessed with great karmic fortune. Having encountered a true teacher, you can enter the right path directly, without wearing out your straw sandals making endless pilgrimages, without wasting your energy following the pipe dream of ascetic religious practice. You are indeed fortunate. Don't let this chance pass by."

A monk said: "I understand what you are telling us. But I have a question. To me, it is like a man wanting to leave a city by fording a river. He must walk a distance. He also needs to use a boat in order to cross the water. Unless he performs those actions, there is no way that he can leave the precincts of the city."

"But here it is. *Right here*," said Bankei. "There's no getting there or not getting there. This is what Zen calls the gate of sudden enlightenment. If you hesitate, you lose it. If you go after it, you draw farther away from it."

In the fifth year of Genroku (1692), when Bankei was staying at the Gyokuryū-ji in Mino Province, he was visited by the Sōtō Zen master Yui'e.[36] Yui'e asked Bankei his opinion of the Five

Ranks of the T'ang master Tōzan Ryōkai,[37] saying: "Tōzan's statements about the Five Ranks, Lord and Vassal, and so on, are tools used by the Dharma teachers in my school. Students travel from one temple to another trying to find some way to penetrate them."

"Tōzan was one of the Zen masters of the past who gained perfect freedom in the exercise of the Dharma," replied Bankei. "Those statements were used as he was dealing carefully with his immediate students. They are just dregs—mere leftovers—of his teaching. They are not essential."

"Do you mean," asked Yui'e, "that the Five Ranks, the Three Essentials, the Three Mysteries, and all the rest are unnecessary? Just meaningless phrases?"[38]

"Any interpretations that are set up and established as truth become meaningless phrases," said Bankei. "It's not a matter of just parroting the patriarchs' words."

A priest visited Bankei at the Gyokuryū-ji in Mino.

"Zen teachers like Daie and Engo used koans to teach their students. Why don't you?" he asked.[39]

"What did the masters who lived before Daie and Engo use?" Bankei replied.

The priest could make no response.

Somewhat later, Bankei said: "Zen teachers lead astray younger generations of students with koans and other constricting verbal complications. The harm they do extends to students far into the future. The sad truth is that for the past three hundred years both teachers and students have mistaken these verbal complications as fixed and unchanging and have regarded them as fundamental to their true selves. They're all of them the same. They pass their lives deceiving both themselves and others. The teachers of the past who were endowed with the Dharma eye acted directly, without relying on Zen stories or koans. They made their students achieve the effortless freedom of marvelous activity through brisk and vital means.

"What do you see today? The men who hold sway as Dharma masters erect stalls, set up shop in them, and proceed to wield their staffs, roar out loud shouts, or throw Zen words and phrases indiscriminately about. Engaging in these pointless and ineffectual acts, imagining them to be the vital activity of the Zen Way, they stimulate their students to ever wilder and more nonsensical behavior, making them completely irresponsible and intemperate and pushing them in the end into a bottomless black pit. How deplorable that the Buddha's Dharma has come to this!"

At the Gyokuryū-ji, a monk asked: "Tokusan and Rinzai taught students through the discipline of the staff and the shout. Why don't you, master?"[40]

"The freedom I've gained with this three-inch drum of mine [my tongue] is all I need when I deal with students," said Bankei. "No one who sails into my port stays very long."

Taking part in the winter retreat of 1690 at the Ryūmon-ji were thirteen hundred priests, representing all of the Buddhist sects. Altogether, there were five or six thousand men and women, from all ranks of society and each of the four classes in the Buddhist community. Bankei frequently ascended to the teaching seat to deliver talks. He was completely surrounded by the great multitude of people. Questions flew at him from every direction like a rain of arrows. He responded to them one by one, every word, every phrase that issued from his mouth came like the swift retort of an echo.

After six or seven such sessions, Bankei said, "Let's stop the questions now. When I get so many questions from individuals like this, I must direct my answers to those people alone, so my words may not reach everyone in the audience. They won't benefit you all."

With that, the questions ceased, and Bankei, speaking with great sincerity and care, proceeded to tell the vast assembly about his teaching of the Unborn.

From that time on, he made the rounds of the training halls each night accompanied by one of his attendants. Fifteen training halls had been readied within the temple precincts. In one of them, Bankei permitted students to come for night interviews. To encourage them, he said: "You should come forward and tell me what is bothering you. Whatever it is, do not hesitate to ask me about it. It is extremely difficult for a student to find a true teacher. You could put on a pair of iron sandals right now and begin a pilgrimage throughout the country. You could go on to China and India. You might make a thousand pilgrimages in a thousand lands, but you would never be able to find another person who could give you the teaching I am giving you now. So don't hesitate. Take it and put it into practice!"

All those present felt an extreme reverence for Bankei. None of them ever forgot the teaching he received. How regrettable that no record was made of this meeting nor of the wonderful golden words uttered by the master as he went from hall to hall responding to his students and answering their questions.

One day when Bankei was at the Kōrin-ji in Edo, a priest of one of the esoteric schools visited him and stayed to listen to one of his talks. Bankei was explaining to the assembly,

"The truth is inescapable: Anger turns you into a fighting spirit, ignorance turns you into an animal."

The priest spoke up: "What you have just stated is different from the central Buddhist idea of the Dharma-body."

"How so?" asked Bankei.

"In the 'Abiding Mind' chapter of the *Dainichi Sutra*, the Buddha says that man's lusting, contentious, ignorant nature is in and of itself the Buddha-nature," the priest declared.[41]

"So is that what you're doing now?" said Bankei.

The priest was speechless.

A priest said: "You only teach about sudden enlightenment and say nothing about gradual training. Didn't Zen master Daie say, 'Sudden enlightenment is the ruling principle, but things are disposed of gradually'?"[42]

"Do you think you can emulate this old priest by putting on Daie's face?" asked Bankei. " 'At one stroke, all previous knowledge is forgotten, without recourse to means or methods.'[43] *See!* Right at this moment, students everywhere in the land are glued fast to words like 'instant enlightenment' and 'gradual realization,' binding themselves up when there's not even any rope, rendering themselves incapable of moving either backward or forward. Ahh, how regrettable that a few phrases uttered by a Buddhist teacher can leave generations crying in confusion at the crossroads."

NOTES TO UNNECESSARY WORDS

1. Jōmyō is the posthumous Zen master title of Itsuzan Sonin (1655–1734). Zen master Reigen is Reigen Shūin (1653–1718). Daikei Kakkō (Sogaku; d. 1719) was a Dharma heir of Setsugai Sotei.

2. A reference to the well-known Zen motto "Direct pointing to the mind of man."

3. The anecdote on which this is based is found in the *Shuramgama Sutra* (Japanese, *Shuryōgon-kyō*), ch. 4. Taishō 19.121b. Yajñādatta took great pleasure in gazing each morning at his reflection in the mirror and became obsessed with the idea of meeting the man he saw there. He began dashing madly about the city looking for him until he finally realized that he was the man and attained peace of mind.

4. This saying, descriptive of the clear and unimpeded working of the Buddha-mind, is found among the records of the T'ang master Jōshū Jūshin (Chao-chou Ts'ung-shen in Chinese). *Dentō-roku*, ch. 10.

5. Bankei resided and taught at the Kōrin-ji during his frequent trips to Edo and the eastern provinces. See Notes to the Dharma Talks, number 55.

6. A saying from the Zen verse *Shinjinmei (Hsin-hsin-ming* in Chinese [Verses on the believing mind]): "The perfect Way is not difficult, only avoid picking and choosing. Just do not love or hate, and it will be perfectly clear and bright. Even a hairbreadth of difference, and it is as distant as heaven from earth."

7. Vimalakirti (Yuima in Japanese). The passage occurs in the "Disciples" chapter of the *Vimalakirti Sutra*. Taishō 14.541a. Mahākātyāyana was one of the Buddha's ten great disciples.

8. This priest refers to *A-ji-kan*, or esoteric meditation on *A-ji*, the first letter of the Sanskrit alphabet and, by extension, the basis of all things. As the object of contemplation, the letter *A* is said to embody the basic principles of Shingon doctrine. Being essentially inherent and not created, it is said to be "originally unborn" *(hompushō)*. The term "gate of eliminating delusion" *(shajō-mon)* refers to the removal of illusion from the unenlightened mind and is used in conjunction with the term "gate of actualizing truth" *(byōtoku-mon)*, which refers to the subsequent expression of fundamental reality.

9. An expression of surprise and admiration.

10. Gutei (Chu-chih; n.d.) was enlightened when his teacher Tenryū

(T'ien-lung; n.d.) raised his finger in the air. Thereafter, he used the same response in answer to all questioners. Cf. *Mumonkan*, case 3; *Hekiganroku*, case 19.

11. Rinzai's use of the shout and Tokusan's use of the staff are proverbial in Zen circles. Funshū Mugō (Fen-chou Wu-yeh; n.d.) responded with the words "No illusions!" *(Makumōzō!)* whenever he was asked a question. *Dentō-roku*, ch. 8. Zuigan Shigen (Jui-yen Shih-yen; n.d.) is known for teaching students using the phrase "Main character" *(Shujinkō;* that is, Original Self). *Mumonkan*, case 12.

12. The island of Hirado, off the northwestern coast of Kyushu, was a fief of the Matsuura clan, whose head, Shigenobu, was a devoted follower of Bankei's. Bankei had one of his disciples reside in the Fumon-ji, and he himself visited on several occasions to conduct retreats. The head priest of the Kōdai-ji at the time is thought to have been Tangen Jichō (n.d.).

13. This account of Chōkei Eryō (Ch'ang-ch'ing Hui-leng; 854–932) appears in the *Zen'en mōgyū (Ch'an-yuan meng-ch'iu)*, a koan collection first published in the Yuan dynasty. Reiun Shigon (Ling-yun Chih-ch'in; n.d.); Seppō Gison (Hsueh-feng I-ts'un; 882–908); Gensha Shibi (Hsuan-sha Shih-pei; 835–908).

14. Kōgen (n.d.) was a high-ranking priest and abbot of the Shinjō-in subtemple of the Ninna-ji, an important Shingon temple in the western part of Kyoto. The Jizō-ji, in Yamashina near Kyoto, was rebuilt by Bankei, who used it as a practice retreat and as a place to recuperate from recurrences of the chronic illness he suffered from during his later life.

15. The *Dainichi Sutra (Dainichi-kyō;* Sanskrit, *Mahāvairocana Sutra)* is the fundamental scripture of the Japanese esoteric schools. The "Abiding Mind" chapter is the *Jūshin-bon*.

16. See note 6.

17. Tenkei Denson (1648–1735) was one of the most important Sōtō teachers of the Edo period, although he was regarded as a maverick in his own sect for his outspoken criticism of some traditional Sōtō

doctrines. His writings were proscribed throughout the Edo period. According to his chronological biography, the *Tenkei oshō nempu*, Tenkei visited Bankei at an inn near Tenkei's temple, the Seikyō-ji near Shizuoka, in 1685, during a stopover Bankei made on one of his trips between the Ryūmon-ji and Edo.

18. Jakua later became Sengaku Soryū (1631–1686) and served as Bankei's successor at the Nyohō-ji in Ōzu.

19. Saichō (762–822), also known as Dengyō Daishi, founded the Japanese Tendai sect, which has its main temple on Mount Hiei, northeast of Kyoto. In Tendai Buddhism, the three teachings are Tendai doctrine, esoteric ritual, and Zen meditation.

20. *Jari*, an abbreviation of *Ajari*, is a term of respect used for ranking priests and teachers in the Tendai and Shingon sects. In the Zen school, it can, as here, be used for ordinary monks.

21. The idea is that a tiger would be even more terrifying with horns.

22. Nothing else is known about this priest.

23. A koan based on words from the *Shuramgama Sutra, ch.* 4. Taishō 19.119. Cf. *Hekiganroku*, case 35.

24. Nothing more is known about this priest.

25. These are two mountain ranges that were said to ring the outermost limits of the world.

26. Kogetsu Zenzai (1667–1751) was a Rinzai priest associated with the Daikō-ji in Hyūga (present Miyazaki prefecture), on the southernmost island of Kyushu. He became one of the most respected masters of his time.

27. The term *buji* ("nothing to do"; "no problems") has several somewhat different connotations and is difficult to translate. In the present context, it describes a person who, having mastered the Buddha Way, has arrived at a place of perfect ease and freedom where there is "nothing left to do."

28. Tesshin Dōin (1593–1680) had studied with the Chinese master Dōsha Chōgen at the Sōfuku-ji in Nagasaki when Bankei was there.

29. This is the Buddha Bhīsma-garjita-svara-rāja (Ion'ō-butsu in Japanese) in the *Lotus Sutra*, who is described as having appeared an inconceivable and immeasurable number of years in the past.

30. Setsugai Sotei (1641–1725) became one of Bankei's leading disciples. He received the honorary Zen master title Daiji Myō'ō Zenji.

31. Daikei Sogaku, Reigen Shūin, and Itsuzan Sonin. See note 1.

32. The Rinzai priest Kengan Zen'etsu (1618–1696), abbot of the Tafuku-ji in Usuki, Bungo Province (present Oita prefecture), was the teacher of Kogetsu Zenzai.

33. This koan, *Gomi kōichi*, derives from words in the *Shuramgama Sutra* and refers to a state where mind and external world exist at all times in a state of perfect suchness. Cf. *Shūmon kattō-shū*, pp. 112–13.

34. Dairyō Sokyō was Bankei's chief heir. See Notes to the Dialogues, number 23.

35. The Nyohō-ji, in the castle town of Ōzu on the island of Shikoku, was one of Bankei's three main temples.

36. The Sōtō priest Yui'e Dōjō (d. 1713) was abbot of the Zen'ō-ji in the province of Owari. He was a member of the brotherhood at the Sōfuku-ji in Nagasaki when Bankei studied there with Dōshoa Chōgen. The Gyokuryū-ji in Mino Province (present Gifu prefecture) was originally a small hermitage Bankei used during the early period of his pilgrimage. It was later made into a large temple.

37. The Five Ranks, or Stages, is a teaching device formulated by the T'ang master Tōzan Ryōkai (Tung-shan Liang-chieh).

38. The Three Essentials *(San'yō)* and Three Mysteries *(Sangen)* are categories found in *The Record of Rinzai*. Their precise significance is not entirely clear.

39. See Notes to the Dialogues, number 12.

40. See Notes to the Dialogues, number 7.

41. See note 15.

42. This statement occurs in the *Letters of Ta-hui* (Japanese, *Daiesho*), letters of religious instruction from Sung master Daie Sōkō (Ta-hui

Tsung-kao) to his students. *Daie-sho*, ed. Araki Kengo (Chikuma, Tokyo, 1969), pp. 36–37. "Things" refers to the afflicting passions; ignorance.

43. These are well-known lines from the enlightenment verse of Kyōgen Chikan (Hsiang-yen Chih-hsien), a ninth-century Chinese monk who attained enlightenment upon hearing a pebble striking a bamboo.

Bibliography
of Works Cited

(Short titles are indicated by capital letters.)

I. RECORDS OF BANKEI'S LIFE AND TEACHING

Titles are given as they appear in *Bankei zenji zenshū* (Complete records of Zen master Bankei C3).

A. Sermons and dialogues

1. *Bankei zenji SEPPŌ* (The sermons of Zen master Bankei). A record of talks, sermons, and dialogues from the great retreat of 1690. A number of different manuscripts exist.

2. *Butchi kōsai zenji HŌGO* (The Dharma words of Zen master Butchi kōsai). A manuscript of dialogues, compiled by Bankei's attendant Itsuzan Sonin.

3. *Genshiken GANMOKU*. Manuscript record of Bankei's sermons, substantially the same as *SEPPŌ* but containing material not found in that work.

4. *ZEIGO* (Unnecessary words). Zen dialogues, compiled fifty years after Bankei's death by a disciple named Sandō Chijō. Contained in the same manuscript as *KYOKKI*.

B. Biographical collections

1. *Bankei daioshō kinen RYAKUROKU* (Brief chronological record of the priest Bankei). Manuscript of anecdotes and sayings by an unidentified disciple.

2. *Bankei oshō GYŌGŌ-KI* (A record of the life of Priest Bankei), compiled the year after Bankei's death by a disciple named Mōsan Soin.

3. *Butchi kōsai zenji gyōgō-RYAKKI* (Brief record of the life of Zen master Butchi kōsai), compiled by Itsuzan Sonin. Contained in the same manuscript as Itsuzan's *HŌGO* collection.

4. *Daihō shōgen kokushi gyōgō-KYOKKI* (Comprehensive records from the life of National Master Daihō Shōgen). Manuscript.

5. *Shōgen kokushi ITSUJIJŌ* (Anecdotes of National Master Shōgen), compiled by Daitei Zenkei, a disciple of Itsuzan Sonin's. Manuscript.

C. Modern editions of the records

1. *Bankei zenji GOROKU* (Recorded sayings of Zen master Bankei), edited by Suzuki Daisetz, Iwanami bunko 2782–2784, Tokyo, first published 1941, still in print.

2. *Bankei zenji HŌGO SHŪ* (Collection of Zen master Bankei's Dharma words), edited by Fujimoto Tsuchishige, Tokyo, Shunjūsha, 1971.

3. *Bankei zenji zenshū* (Complete records of Zen master Bankei), edited by AKAO Ryūji, Daizō shuppan, Tokyo, 1976. Contains all the works listed above in A and B.

These are the three main editions of Bankei's records. The one by Suzuki, for many years the standard, gives a complete text of the sermons, Itsuzan's *Hōgo*, the *Zeigo*, and three of the biographical collections. It has been superseded by the editions of Fujimoto and Akao. Fujimoto offers a well-edited text of the sermons, Itsuzan's *Hōgo*, and three of the biographical collections. The Akao edition, the first attempt to bring together all the above material in one volume, is now the principal edition of Bankei's records.

II. MODERN WORKS ON BANKEI IN JAPANESE

1. *Bankei daioshō* (Great priest Bankei), NAGAI Sekihō, Seikyōsha, Tokyo, 1926. Selections from Bankei's records.

2. *Bankei kokushi no kenkyū* (A study of National Master Bankei), FUJIMOTO Tsuchishige, Shunjūsha, Tokyo, 1971. Detailed study of the life records; chronologically arranged.

3. *Bankei no FUSHŌ ZEN* (Bankei's Unborn Zen), Suzuki Daisetz, Kōbundō, Tokyo, 1940; vol. I of Suzuki's *Complete Works*. With no. 7, still the best study of Bankei's Zen.

4. *Bankei Zen no kenkyū* (STUDIES of Bankei Zen), edited by Suzuki Daisetz and Furuta Shōkin. Sankibō, Tokyo, 1942. Contains essays by Suzuki and six other well-known scholars and Zen priests.

5. *Dōgen, Bankei, Hakuin no ryōbyō tetsugaku* (The philosophy of treating illness of Dōgen, Bankei, and Hakuin), AOKI Shigeru, Dō-shinbō, Tokyo, 1943.

6. *Zen bunka* (Zen culture), periodical, nos. 10–11, April 1958. Special combined issue devoted to Bankei.

7. *Zenshisō-shi KENKYŪ: Bankei Zen* (Studies in the history of Zen thought: Bankei Zen), Suzuki Daisetz, Iwanami, Tokyo, first published in 1943; in vol. I of Suzuki's *Complete Works*.

III. OTHER WORKS

1. *The Analects of Confucius,* Arthur Waley, Allen & Unwin, London, 1938.

2. *The Christian Century in Japan, 1549–1650.* C. R. Boxer, University of California Press, Berkeley, 1951.

3. *Daigu ihō* (The calligraphy of Priest Daigu), Zen bunka ken-kyūsho, Kyoto, 1970.

4. *GUDŌ* (Zen master Gudō), Itō Kokan, Shunjūsha, Tokyo, 1969.

5. *HEKIGANROKU* (Chinese, *Pi-yen lu*; The blue cliff records) by Engo Kokugon (Chinese, Yuan-wu K'o-ch'in), Taishō 48.

6. *History of Japan,* 3 vols. Engelbert KAEMPFER, James Maclehose and Sons, Glasgow, 1906.

7. *History of Japan, 1615–1867.* George Sansom, Stanford University Press, Stanford, Calif., 1963.

8. *Keitoku DENTŌ-ROKU* (Chinese, *Ching-te ch'uan-teng lu*); The record of the lamp of the Keitoku era), compiled by Dōgen (Chinese, Tao-yuan), Taishō 55.

BIBLIOGRAPHY

9. *Living by Zen*, D. T. [Daisetz] Suzuki, Sanseido, Tokyo, 1949.

10. *MUMONKAN* (Chinese, *Wu-men kuan*; The gateless barrier) by Mumon Ekai (Chinese, Wu-men Hui-k'ai), Taishō 48.

11. *MYŌSHIN-JI*, Ogisu Jundō, Tōyōbunka-sha, Kyoto, 1977.

12. *The Record of Lin-chi*, translated by Ruth Sasaki, Institute for Zen Studies, Kyoto, 1975.

13. *Shūmon Kattō-shū*, edited by Kajitani Sonin, Hōzōkan, Kyoto, 1982.

14. *TEIKAN zen-ni* (The Zen nun Teikan), Fujimoto Tsuchishige, Shunjūsha, Tokyo, 1977.

15. *Tenkei nempu* (Chronological biography of Tenkei), Jikishi Gentan, Kyoto, 1767.

16. *Zen Comments on the Mumonkan*, Zenkei SHIBAYAMA, Mentor Books, New York, 1974.